# THE GREATEST BATTLES OF WORLD WAR II

### A World at War:
### World War II Battles That
### Shaped the Course of History

Alexander L. Sheppard

# TABLE OF CONTENTS

# INTRODUCTION

When the Second World War broke out on September 1 of 1939, it would soon evolve into the greatest conflict in human history. At its peak, it involved twice as many nations across the globe than were involved in the First World War and far more global casualties. Many in the early to mid-1930s who foresaw war on the horizon knew that another massive conflict would be the worst that Europe or the rest of the world had yet seen. Still, few understood the true extent of what was to come by the end of the decade. It is difficult to say with any certainty how severe the human cost was across the world as a direct or indirect result of World War II, but the estimates themselves are breathtaking. Between 35 million and 60 million are believed to have been victims of the conflict, which lasted from 1939 until 1945 (Royde-Smith, n.d.). Needless to say, a tremendous amount of bloodshed and loss of life was achieved in just six years. Also, unlike the First World War, this conflict was one with genuinely global implications, with one side being bent on complete European conquest and global hegemony.

Aside from just the scope and scale of the death, it was also the most inhumane and brutal war that humanity had wrought upon itself. It was the first massive war where the murder of civilians was a *main objective of the conflict*, rather than an unfortunate byproduct, or so-called collateral damage. The elimination of European Jews was not an afterthought for the German Nazi Party when they began their wars of conquest. Rather, it was what motivated them. Importantly, the Holocaust was not confined to Germany proper—it followed the Nazi war machine wherever it went—France, Poland, Bohemia and Moravia, the Soviet Union, and elsewhere. All of their Jewish communities came under threat from the Nazi racial ideology and policy. Of course, it was not only Jews who were the targets of intentional civilian killings. Gays and lesbians, the mentally and physically handicapped, the Romani people of Eastern Europe, and even communists (or suspected communists) could be murdered wholesale under the direction of the German Reich. After the Wehrmacht (German army) invaded the Soviet Union and began their push into the Russian city of Stalingrad in 1942, the entire population of the city had been condemned. As recorded by German high command: "the führer [Adolf Hitler] orders that on entry into the city of Stalingrad the entire male population should be liquidated, since Stalingrad with its thoroughly communist population of a million, is particularly dangerous" (quoted in Clairmont, 2003).

Eastern Europe and Asia (specifically China) suffered the worst of the casualties, without question. As the Wehrmacht rolled across the Soviet border into the Russian heartland, Soviet civilians bore the brunt of the force. Millions of innocent people in their path died, and pushing the Germans back out took the lives of millions more Soviet soldiers. On the other side of the world, the slaughter was being carried out by the Imperial Japanese Army (IJA), an ally of the Wehrmacht over the course of the war. The primary victims here were the Chinese. Again, this included millions of civilians as well as the armies of both the Kuomintang and the Chinese Communist Party, who were embroiled in a civil war with each other before uniting against the Japanese invaders. The civilian death toll and brutality on the part of the IJA has led the massacres in China to be known as the "Asian Holocaust" (Todd, 2016). Despite the obvious implied comparison to the conflict in Europe, many view the war in Asia and the Pacific as a separate conflict. Indeed, many of the conflicts occurring around the globe at the time were not directly tied to each other, and some were only tangentially related, such as the Soviet Union's war against Finland. Still, these conflicts across the globe all influenced each other to varying degrees, and all are lumped into the overarching Second World War.

In reality, the origins of the Second World War can be found several decades prior to its outbreak, and perhaps even longer. For our purposes though, we can take Adolf Hitler's rise to power as, at least, an initial point from which to begin. Hitler, a veteran of the First World War, began rising to national prominence around the early 1920s when the political party he led, the *Deutsche Arbeiterpartei* (also known as the German Workers Party) was reorganized around the ideology of National Socialism. The party added *Nationalsozialistische* to its name and became what we know today as the Nazi party. Despite its name, the Nazi party had almost negligible socialist influence and no socialist policies. In fact, Hitler and the party leadership were vehemently anti-communist, viewing Soviet-style socialism as tied to Judaism, and therefore, antithetical to Western civilization. The "socialism" in National Socialism was almost certainly placed there intentionally in order to garner the support of Germany's working-class poor (Fitzpatrick & Moses, 2018). The truth is that actual socialism, in addition to the Jewish population, was emphasized as a dire threat to the German fatherland and its people.

Hitler continued to grow in popularity and secured his position at the top of Nazi leadership, building a kind of cult-of-personality around himself by the mid-1920s. At the time, Hitler wanted the Nazis to seize power by force from what he viewed as a weak Weimar Republican government (the Weimar Republic refers to the German government that held power between the end of World War I in 1918 and the beginning of the Nazi reign in 1933). To that end, in November of 1923, Hitler and thousands of Nazi members and supporters marched to a beer hall in Munich in an attempt to seize significant control of the government and to install leading Nazi officials in high-ranking government positions. Hitler and his brownshirts (the nickname for Hitler's supporters at the time, who wore brown uniforms, a reference to Italian dictator Benito Mussolini's "blackshirt" supporters) demanded the support of local leaders in Munich and attempted to seize control of key facilities in the city. There was a confrontation between police and armed brownshirts, at one point, while the Nazis were marching toward the center of the city, and it left several Nazi leaders shot, Hitler injured, and the brownshirts routed. Shortly after, Hitler was arrested, subsequently convicted, and "the putsch had come to an ignominious end" (Evans, 2004).

Despite being convicted of treasonous acts against Germany, Adolf Hitler would spend less than a year in prison. But it was enough time for him to write a book and have it edited by fellow imprisoned Nazis. The manifesto was titled *Mein Kampf*, translating to "My Struggle" or "My Battle," and in it he espoused the ideals of National Socialism and put the blame for all of Germany's woes on a combined Jewish-Soviet plot for domination. The tone was violent and what was being called for was clear enough: the extermination of Germany's Jewish population and the eradication of communist influences. Upon Hitler's release from prison, he was more popular than ever. *Mein Kampf* was gaining traction in anti-Semitic and nationalist circles in Germany, and Hitler's arrest and imprisonment after the failed putsch in Munich had turned him into something of a martyr. Having sacrificed himself for the German people, Hitler's support grew significantly. In light of the failed putsch, the Nazis would from this point participate in elections and attempt to seize power politically rather than in a coup. Despite the rise of Hitler's personal popularity, the Nazi party still suffered a terrible defeat in the 1928 elections, but when another election was called in 1930, it was a major victory with the Nazis winning the second highest number of seats in the German Reichstag. Importantly, the German communists also secured a considerable increase in seats.

The success of both of these parties was in large part due to the 1929 economic crisis which ushered in the Great Depression. The Depression had global reach and the German economy, which had recently begun to recover from the effects of the disastrous Treaty of Versailles, was not spared. The Treaty of Versailles was the peace deal that Germany was compelled to sign to end the First World War and it forced the country to disarm, pay massive war reparations to the victorious nations, and accept full responsibility for the outbreak of war. The German economy suffered massively as a result, and many felt disgraced, humiliated, and betrayed by the German government that signed the treaty. Hitler was able to seize upon this resentment amongst Germans and vowed, as a main tenet of National Socialism, to reverse the injustice done by Versailles. Because of the United States' economic plan for Germany, which relieved some of the stress brought by the war reparations, the country had been recovering. However, when the Depression struck, the economic crisis was renewed. The federal election of the following year was centered on economic issues, and the Nazi party offered both scapegoats and fantastic promises. Germany was a country primed for political extremism. After another election in 1932 ended without forming a majority government, German President Paul von Hindenberg came under intense pressure from the elites in Germany, including leaders of banking and heavy industry, to make Hitler the Chancellor. Seeing few options to avoid a potential civil war, he agreed. In the first month of 1933, Adolf Hitler gained control of the German government.

Although much of the story of World War II begins with Hitler's rise to power, the majority of the ideas he represented were not new. For one thing, virulent anti-Semitism was already many centuries old in Germany by this point. Martin Luther (1483–

1546), the father of German Protestantism, preached hatred against the Jews in his later years, and Catholic church leaders often condemned Jews as the murderers of Christ. Contemporary German anti-Semitism was especially fierce after 1899, during which time racialist Social Darwinism, also known as scientific racism, was popular in much of the West. Proponents of Social Darwinism view the world through a racial lens and see it engaged in a struggle between racial groups, some superior to others. Thus, Hitler's conception of a German Aryan "master race," destined to dominate all others, was not a unique invention in the 1930s.

The concept of lebensraum, another tenet of Hitler's National Socialism, was also not new. Lebensraum, literally meaning "living space," was the notion that the German volk (people) were expanding and multiplying, and therefore needed more physical space to occupy to avoid population density. Most of this lebensraum was to be obtained at the expense of Eastern Europe, as we will see. The concept was neither new, nor unique to Germany. It had been advocated for in the German empire and Weimar Republic long before Hitler's rise to power, and the Italian fascists had their own version, *spazio vitale*, holding the same meaning. For Mussolini, *spazio vitale*'s ultimate goal was the reclamation of the territory of the former Roman Empire. Indeed, much of what Hitler said and did was not unfamiliar to Germans. What it took for these ideas to become so powerful was a strong speaker, someone to embody the rage Germans collectively felt and successfully channel it toward his own goals.

After Hitler's ascent to the Chancellorship, a series of events in Germany and abroad inched the world closer and closer to the brink of war. Just one month later, on February 27 of 1933, the German Reichstag (parliamentary building) in Berlin was severely damaged in a blaze. After the government made the determination that it was intentional arson, the Nazis seized the opportunity to claim a communist coup was underway and that emergency dictatorial powers were required to prevent it. The resulting Reichstag Fire Decree gave the Nazis unprecedented unilateral power. A number of conflicts in the mid-1930s also provided important training grounds for the fascist militaries, which for Nazi Germany's newly rebuilt Wehrmacht, was vital.

In 1935, Mussolini's fascists invaded the East African nation of Ethiopia in order to unite Italy's African colonies and to exact revenge on the Ethiopians who humiliated the Italians in a military defeat decades earlier. The fighting was finished by 1937 with an Italian victory, and more important than the experience that Italian soldiers gained was the diplomatic response. The western allied nations had only mild criticism of the invasion, and this gave the impression of a weak-willed spirit in Britain and France. Perhaps, then, the Nazis and their allies should continue to push their limits. In 1936 another conflict broke out that garnered Europe's attention: the Spanish civil war. On one side was Francisco Franco who, like Hitler and Mussolini, was a fascist. On the other, an alliance of republic democrats, communists, and anarchists. Both Germans and Italians sent expeditionary forces to aid Franco between 1936 and 1939, again earning valuable warfare experience. In the end, Franco's fascists were victorious. Hitler and Mussolini were emboldened, and the global fascist movement claimed another major victory.

While these wars were raging, the ideology of pan-Germanism grew rapidly. This was the concept that all Germans, regardless of which country they found themselves citizens of, belonged with Germans and within the German Reich. Of course, both pan-Germanism and lebensraum necessarily involved military conquest, both to expand the area that Germans could live in and to incorporate neighboring territory in which large numbers of ethnic Germans found themselves. One of the major steps toward the goal of bringing foreign Germans under the Reich was the proposed absorption of Austria into Germany. Austria too had a National Socialist Nazi party holding a degree of political power, and the question of German-Austrian unification had been on the table for a long time. Through various scheming efforts, Hitler was able to get a telegram (purporting to be from the Austrian government) sent to Germany with a request for military aid. Hitler obliged the phony telegram by deploying the military on March 12 of 1938 and secured an agreement for full annexation the next day. After a staged referendum the next month, Austria, with all her ethnically German citizens, was incorporated into the Reich. It was known as the Anschluss or "Unification," and inspired fear, but not action, throughout Europe.

The diplomatic, yet heavy-handed territorial gains did not end for Germany with the Anschluss. Later, in September of 1938, Hitler had his eyes on the Sudeten region of neighboring Czechoslovakia, another region dominated by ethnic Germans. Earlier in the year, German forces and Germans living in Czechoslovakia had begun making incursions into the border and the Sudetenland region, and Hitler demanded that the Czechoslovak government cede the territory to the Reich. Czech president Edvard Beneš was staunchly opposed, and for good reason. The Czechs had been building up extensive fortifications along the border with Germany in the mountainous areas of the Sudetenland since 1935 in response to German rhetoric and saber-rattling. If the Sudetenland were to be given over to the Reich, Czechoslovakia would lose the mountains, which were more easily defended, and the country would be laid bare to await a German invasion. Further, their enemies would be in control of the very defensive structures they had built to keep them out.

Despite the Czechoslovak opposition to German demands, the Allied nations simply wanted the matter resolved, and requested that the Czechs hand over the territory. The dispute escalated as Hitler became more aggressive, and the matter threatened to be the initial outbreak of the next World War, which world leaders had been trying to avoid since 1918. At the time, France had a pre-existing military alliance with Czechoslovakia and, in the case of a full-scale invasion, would be obliged to join the war effort. Then, Britain would have little choice but to send troops to the continent. Needless to say, this had to be avoided at all costs.

So, in September of 1938, world leaders met in the German city of Munich to make a last attempt to deter a full invasion of Czechoslovakia. Those in attendance included French Prime Minister Edouard Daladier, British Prime Minister Neville Chamberlain, as well as Hitler and Mussolini. Notably, neither Edvard Beneš nor any Czechoslovak delegates were invited to the meeting. Without input from the Beneš government or its people, the four leaders signed the Munich Agreement which provided for the annexation of the Sudetenland by Germany. In exchange, Hitler and the Nazis were to abandon all further ambitions of territorial expansion at the expense of its European neighbors. After all, Hitler had added both Austrian and Czechoslovak Germans to the Reich and should have been satisfied.

The agreement was well received in Britain. The British were a people eager to avoid sending another generation of young men off to war, the scars of the First World War still fresh in the collective memory. The French, too, were eager to avoid another confrontation with Germany, a country with whom France had a historic rivalry. Despite the promises made and the celebrations taking place in Britain and elsewhere, Hitler had no intention of ceasing German expansion. The Allies had repeatedly backed off and given in to his demands. Why should he stop at the Sudetenland?

Tension on the home front was also escalating in Germany in 1938. Anti-Semitism had been growing steadily more aggressive until it erupted in violence and chaos. In November of 1938, Germans across the country and in the new territory Austria went on a spree of violent hate crimes against German Jews, their homes, synagogues, and businesses. During the night of the 9th–10th of that month, tens of thousands of Jews were arrested without cause and taken away by the Nazis. To add to these crimes, the Nazis, in the aftermath, forced German Jews to pay a reparation tax for the crimes they had supposedly committed against the German *volk*. Among these crimes was the recent assassination of a German diplomat in France. The assassination was carried out by a young

Polish Jew whose family had recently been forcibly deported from their homes in Germany.

The Nazis claimed that the outburst of violence against Jews was the impulsive reaction of the collective German people in response to the assassination, as well as other imagined evils. In reality, though, the spasm of violence which came to be known as *kristallnacht* or "night of broken glass" was carefully planned and meticulously detailed. Planning and execution were carried out largely by Nazi party members as well as members of the *sturmabteilung* (SA), the Nazis' first paramilitary wing. Above all, *kristallnacht* proved beyond doubt that the Nazis were serious about their racial policies and that no Jews in Europe would be safe if Germany continued to expand.

The policy of appeasement that the European Allies had pursued since Hitler began making his demands has been the subject of debate. Appeasement represented the belief that as long as Hitler was given enough of what he wanted to keep him happy, he and the German people would eventually stop making demands once they felt that they had received justice. Of course, this proved disastrously false. Many historians see the appeasement of Hitler as a tragic or foolish mistake, and imply that the leaders of the Allies, namely Chamberlain, were blind to Hitler's intentions (after the outbreak of war, Chamberlain would be replaced by Winston Churchill). In reality, leadership in both Britain and France knew that a war involving Germany was very likely at some point in the future. The policy of appeasement was not guided by a naive belief that Hitler would eventually stop making demands, but rather was pursued primarily as a way to indefinitely postpone the outbreak of war between the Nazis and the Allies. Both Britain and France were unprepared for large-scale war and their militaries needed significant time to arm and re-equip their forces to be able to stand a chance against Germany on the continent. In this way, the policy was at least partially successful, but the beginning of a massive conflict appeared more and more likely by the day.

By the end of May 1939, Hitler and Mussolini had signed the so-called Pact of Steel, which officially bound their two nations in a military alliance. Then, in the summer of that year, Hitler and Josef Stalin, leader of the Soviet Union, signed the Molotov-Ribbentrop Pact (named for the Soviet and German Foreign Affairs Ministers, Vyacheslav Molotov and Joachim von Ribbentrop, respectively), a non-aggression agreement between the fascist and communist states. It included provisions to carve up Eastern Europe between the two large nations, and Poland was set to be their first joint target. It would also allow the Soviet Union to pursue their own expansionist goals without fear of German interference. Most importantly though, the Molotov-Ribbentrop Pact ensured that Hitler would be able to wage war against the Western Allies without the fear of a second front opening in the east. With these pacts and alliances in place, Hitler and his allies were prepared for war.

So, the stage was set for the outbreak of something massive. Unfortunately, even the horrors of the First World War could not have prepared the people of Europe entirely for the destruction that was to come. The course of the war itself, however, was not nearly the only concern on the minds of Europeans and others. As destructive and violent as the conflict would be, the fate that awaited the world, if the democratic powers were to fall, promised to be even more terrible. The Axis powers of Germany and Italy (and soon, the militaristic, fascist-esque Japan) had intended on something far grander than regional domination, and with Germany as the chief partner in the alliance, the ideologies of Nazism would surely prevail. Without any entities strong enough to challenge them, the fascist powers would be free to enforce their racial policies as they expanded their empires across the world. The global extermination of Jews and countless other ethnic groups that the Nazis considered inferior would certainly have soon followed, as well as the likely end of democracy as a powerful governing institution. But how was this future avoided? How did the German war machine, which had continuously outclassed coalitions of its neighbors in combat at the outset of the war, ultimately crumble before it was able to subdue the European continent permanently? And how was fascism, a popular political movement, destroyed?

In order to be answered, these questions require a close look at what actually happened on the ground over the course of the war. It also requires a wide field of vision, one that takes the global scale of the fighting and developments across the world into account. From the Dutch fields to the streets of Paris, the skies over London to the deserts of North Africa, the frozen Russian steppes to the countless, insignificantly small islands scattered throughout the Pacific—the battles that took place here and elsewhere between 1939 and 1945 defined the future.

More than the politicians and stay-at-home generals, the course of history depended chiefly on those that were on the ground, fighting the war. Moscow and Stalingrad, Pearl Harbor and Midway, Alamein and Sicily—the outcomes of these battles and others had massive reverberations which lasted the duration of the war. Not only did they help determine the outcomes of future battles within the Second World War, but they also determined the state of the world after its end. For this reason, the battles themselves must be understood. Aside from just the logistics, strategies, and outcomes of these battles, we must understand why they took place and exactly what was at stake for each of them. What distinguishes, for example, a slow siege of Moscow from a skirmish in the deserts of Libya, aside from simply the number of casualties inflicted on each army? This book will take a look at all of the most important battles of the Second World War, paying close attention to the details that help us answer these questions. A coherent narrative of these battles, combined with an understanding of how they shaped and influenced each other and the overall trajectory of the war, can help us understand how World War II was more than just a war of conquest and politics—it was also a war for morality and the survival of democratic freedoms. These are the most important battles of World War II and all of modern human history, and they are what ensured this survival.

# CHAPTER 1:
# THE WESTERN FRONT OPENS

## The Battle of France

After years of the Allied nations' policy of appeasement failing to satisfy the ambitions of Nazi leader Adolf Hitler, most soon realized that the outbreak of large-scale war was inevitable, and by 1939, perhaps imminent. In March of that year, Hitler had gone back on his word and forsook the promises made in the Munich Agreement of 1938. The Wehrmacht had entered Czechoslovakia, occupied the country, and eventually installed puppet governments in the territory, including the Protectorate of Bohemia and Moravia, and the Slovak State. In response to this, the Western Allies issued a guarantee to Poland, another nation on which the Nazis had set their sights. It bound both Britain and France to aid in the preservation of Polish sovereignty. In other words, war against the Polish meant war against the British, the French, and all their colonies. Unlike with Czechoslovakia, the Allies were determined to keep their promise. The time for giving in to German demands and appeasing Hitler's ambitions was over, and a line in the sand had been drawn. Poland would be the final straw.

### The Fall of Poland and the Phony War

To Hitler, who had become accustomed to getting what he wanted so long as he yelled loud enough, the Allied guarantee of Polish sovereignty apparently mattered little. The Molotov-Ribbentrop Pact had given Hitler even more assurances that Poland would be an easy conquest, and likely would be accomplished well before either Britain or France could do anything about it. By the time the Allies would be prepared to fight, Poland would already be won, and Germany would refocus the military toward the west. So, on the first day of September 1939, in accordance with the military agreement between Germany and the Soviet Union, Poland was invaded—first by Germany, with the Soviet Union following suit and invading from the east two weeks later.

Just two days after the initial invasion, on September 3, the Allies honored their alliance and issued a formal declaration of war against Germany. Once again, Europe had become embroiled in a war of alliances (though notably, Italy was not yet involved in open conflict). Interestingly, the Allies did not declare war on the Soviet Union when they too invaded Poland, likely correctly realizing that they would be taking on two giants that they could not hope to defeat together. The fact that the Allies did not commence hostilities with the Soviet Union at the beginning of World War II had massive implications for future events, as we will see.

Despite the declaration of war, Hitler was correct in his estimation. Geographically speaking, it was infeasible for either Britain or France to successfully defend Poland from a German invasion. They were simply too far away, and without any significant troop presence within the country, it would fall entirely before any Allied relief showed up. And so, Poland was doomed, and the government soon capitulated. On September 28, less than a month after German troops stepped across the border, the Polish government surrendered, unable to withstand the assault on the capital city of Warsaw.

The next day, both the Germans and Soviets honored their pact and partitioned the Polish territory between them along the Bug River, which ran, roughly, down the center of the country. The successful conquest was an important win for Hitler, who had now eliminated the last eastern ally of the British and French who could have a realistic chance at sandwiching Germany. Hitler could now focus all his efforts to the west, where the Allies, in the meantime, had made no significant progress. For Stalin, the victory and acquisition of Polish territory was also important. Despite the Molotov-Ribbentrop Pact, a German invasion of the Soviet Union was still very much a realistic possibility, and Stalin in particular foresaw a coming conflict. In this event, securing a buffer zone of Polish territory would allow the Soviets more time to prepare and mobilize before German invaders would be able to reach Russia proper. Scattered resistance still continued in Poland after the official surrender, but this had been quelled within the first week of October. Poland had fallen, and sadly, Polish Jews were to experience some of the worst horrors of the war.

Since sending troops to Poland would have, ultimately, been pointless, the British government instead sent their expeditionary forces directly across the English Channel into France and the Low Countries (Belgium and the Netherlands), where the Allies anticipated the next attacks would be launched. While the Low Countries were not expected to stand for long on their own, British and French troops were relied on to carry the weight of the Allied powers.

France's military mindset at the beginning of the war could best be described as highly defensive and precautious. Due mostly to France's memory of Germany's aggressiveness from the First World War and because of the two nations' historic rivalry, France intended to wage a steady and defensive war. This mentality had resulted in the construction of the famous "Maginot Line" over the course of the 1930s. It was an extensive, heavily fortified defensive line built across the length of the French-German border. While the Line served to deter German invasions into France, its true purpose was to entice Germany to attack France via the Low Countries to the north instead. This way, French forces would be able to meet the German advance and fight them in Belgium and the Netherlands instead of on French soil. The Line was indeed formidable, and it made direct German invasion into the French homeland impractical.

Very soon after the Allies declared war against Germany, French troops made brief incursions into Germany, pushing past the Maginot Line into the German Saarland region. The goal was to relieve Poland by forcing German troops back across the country rather than to actually conquer and hold German land. Fearing that a major defeat and subsequent retreat back to France could shatter the Maginot Line, French military command preferred instead to draw them through the northern corridor. Unfortunately for the French, the fall of Poland was rapid and the redeployment of German troops to the western front occurred sooner than expected. The French were quickly forced to abandon the minor invasion and retreat back to the French side of the Maginot Line. What followed was an eight-month period of hardly any open conflict, a period that came to be known as the Phony War.

But what caused the opposing armies to come to a virtual standstill in the middle of open war? From the French point of view, they were not willing to make further incursions into Germany and were instead committed to waiting for the chance to repel an invasion force, and so they maintained their defensive position at the Maginot Line. The Germans, on the other hand, did not need to rush an invasion of France, nor were they yet committed to an all-out war against their neighbors. In fact, Hitler was still maintaining hope that he could sign a peace deal with Britain and avoid a conflict with them altogether. After all, Hitler apparently respected the nation and viewed the Anglo-Saxons as an advanced race that could potentially co-exist with German Aryans. Winston Churchill, however, was no longer interested in playing along with the German demands and requests. He refused truce offers from Hitler even in the face of Italian pleas for a peaceful end to the conflict. It seems that Churchill, by this point, was as committed to a Total War in Europe and across the world as Hitler was. Still, the Nazis delayed fighting or invading the two largest Allied nations until their patience wore out. On May 9 of 1940, Hitler gave the order to invade France, and the Phony War ended the next day.

### The Manstein Plan

Just as the French had hoped, the initial German assault was conducted through the Low Countries. The plans for the eventual assault against the Western Allies had changed and been revised several times prior to invasion, but the final version consisted of the speedy conquest of the Netherlands and Belgium before pushing rapidly toward the French capital of Paris. The French had anticipated this but unfortunately for Paul Reyaud, the French Prime Minister who had recently taken power from the resigned Daladier, the German invasion through the Low Countries also served as an important diversion. The Wehrmacht understood that the French would expect this assault but needed to take them by surprise in order to ensure a speedy victory.

To that end, the Manstein Plan, which called for a much lighter Netherlands and Belgium assault, was developed. Instead, the primary invasion force was to enter France through the thickly forested Ardennes region around the borders of France, Belgium, Germany, and Luxembourg. During the French planning stage of the invasion, the Ardennes region had been disregarded as a non-viable route for German invasion. The terrain was rough and unsuitable for mass deployment, especially for tank or armored units. This was, in fact, what made it a perfect invasion point for Hitler, so long as his units could make it through without being bogged—ultimately, it was a gamble. As a result of overlooking the Ardennes region, the French army had left the area almost completely unmanned and undefended. Worse still, the thick forest would provide excellent air cover to conceal the advancing forces within. So, during the opening days of the Battle of France, the fighting in the Low Countries provided a smokescreen for the heavy German panzer tank divisions as they swiftly yet carefully cut through the Ardennes Forest on their way to flank and surround Allied forces.

Meanwhile, the fighting in the Low Countries was disastrous for the Allies. The Netherlands was almost immediately overwhelmed and surrendered just four days after the initial invasion. Belgium's King Leopold ordered a full surrender by May 28, and Luxembourg, a tiny country on Belgium's south-eastern border, capitulated with barely a shot fired in its defense. France also performed much more poorly than expected and suffered for it. This was a surprise to many, as France's military was very highly regarded in the pre-war years.

In 1940, they learned that war had changed. France's army was governed by an outdated military doctrine as well as old-school generals who were anticipating another World War I scenario with long, drawn out trench warfare which moved the front line inches at a time. What they got instead was the Wehrmacht's blitzkrieg tactics, characterized by heavy and continuous artillery, highly mobile warfare, and rapid advance and deployment. It did not take long for the confused French forces to be routed and forced to fall back toward the French border. The French military had also made another fatal miscalculation. While Hitler remade and revolutionized the German air force (known as the Luftwaffe) in the lead-up to the war, the French apparently still viewed aerial combat and support as a secondary or even tertiary aspect of warfare. This meant it would be easy for the Germans, who had given their air force a central role within their overall offensive plan, to provide their troops with air support without heavy interference from the French. Perhaps worst of all, France's tank-busting equipment was outdated and in far too short supply to defend against the German panzers when they inevitably broke out of the Ardennes Forest and began the drive toward the French heartland, which they did on May 13.

After successfully navigating the Ardennes, the German tank divisions sped toward their goal, easily occupying the French town of Sedan after the defenders—some of the most inexperienced troops the French military had to offer—abandoned it and retreated across the Meuse River. The Germans would have to cross a river with defenders waiting on the other side if they were to have any hope of encircling the French, and they would need to do it before reinforcements arrived. What followed was one of the most famous cases of the use of the Wehrmacht's blitzkrieg, which had been developed and perfected by German general Heinz Guderian just prior to the war. The still underprepared defenders couldn't survive the advance, and the Germans successfully crossed the Meuse and penetrated into the French interior.

Army Group A, the invasion force tasked with the Ardennes route, made such great use of Guderian's tactics that they eliminated the chance of the invasion devolving into a war of attrition—German advance was assured. The panzer divisions quickly moved north to capture French ports along the coast of the English Channel, and they quickly surrounded the Allied soldiers who had been pushed back from the Low Countries. By May 21, the Wehrmacht had reached its goal. This state of affairs was a calamity, but French morale had already plummeted days before this. On May 15, shortly after the German victory at Sedan and just *five days* after the invasion began, Reynaud phoned Churchill and informed him that, in his view, hope was lost, and the war was over.

## Dunkirk

When German forces arrived at the northern coastal area, French and British forces were trapped on all sides around the city of Dunkirk at the extreme northern tip of France. Germans were everywhere and their backs were against the ocean. Hundreds of thousands of Allied troops were cornered and helpless, awaiting what many thought would be an inevitable slaughter. It is true that the combined force of the Wehrmacht and Luftwaffe could have launched an all-out assault and destroyed what remained of the northern French army and British Expeditionary force. But by some incredible stroke of good fortune, no assault happened. Seemingly without reason, the German forces simply held their position around Dunkirk while the remainder of the invasion force continued to push into the interior. As it turned out, Hitler, acting on the advice of some of his generals (namely, Gerd von Rundstedt and Günther von Kluge) had ordered the advancing troops to halt for three days, set to begin again on May 26. Explanations as to why Hitler decided to pause the assault on Dunkirk are varied and still debated to this day, but what is certain is that the halt was absolutely critical not just to the fate of the soldiers stranded at Dunkirk, but to the entire war effort.

On the one hand, Hitler and some of his advisors and generals were concerned that an all-out assault on Dunkirk, if it went poorly, could lead to a massive Allied breakthrough in the German line, compromising Germany's much-needed tank divisions as well as their strategic position. After all, the Allied forces at Dunkirk, while they were cornered, were still considerable in number. If the Allies repelled an aggressive assault, it could spell doom for the entire invasion of France which, so far, had been executed perfectly by the Germans. Hitler had also assured Hermann Göring, high commander of the German air force, that he would allow his Luftwaffe to deal the finishing blow to Dunkirk, considering the terrain was unfavorable to the tank warfare which had proved so successful up to this point. Göring also gave assurances that he would be able to prevent any attempt of escape from Dunkirk, so Hitler needn't worry about delaying the assault. Further, it appears that Hitler was more concerned with pressing forward to Paris in order to deal a deathblow to the French government and gain a prestigious victory than he was with finishing off the troops at Dunkirk. Finally, it's also likely that Hitler was still holding out hope that, after France had been utterly defeated, he would be able to negotiate peace with Churchill and the British. Delaying the annihilation of the Expeditionary Forces would be beneficial in this regard.

*British Prime Minister Winston Churchill*

Whatever the main motivating factor was for the halt, it provided the Allies with a major opportunity to stage a desperate and daring evacuation from the French coastal city. It lay not far from the British coast, and a total evacuation, while risky, was not infeasible. The three days of respite allowed for the proper co-ordination of the escape, and the Allies enlisted the help of civilian vessels to accomplish the task. The evacuation, codenamed Operation Dynamo, lasted several days and saw heavy casualties, with tens of thousands killed or taken prisoner. Still, it was an overall success. The massive operation allowed for over 300,000 Allied troops to make their way across the channel to Britain (Summerfield, 2010). Many French soldiers had given their lives to ensure the safe transport of their British allies, and Dunkirk itself was also sacrificed—by the end of the battle, the city was lying in ruin.

At a time when Allied morale was dangerously low, Dunkirk was a rejuvenation. More than anything, the fact that a retreat accompanied with heavy deaths was hailed as a great victory speaks to the state of mind of the British and French. Losses had been so great and the outlook so bleak that not being *completely* destroyed was cause for celebration. Indeed, it was a great propaganda victory for Churchill, and Dunkirk almost immediately became part of British military legend as a lesson in the value of courage and spirit. But the celebration of Dunkirk was not entirely without reason. The rescue of hundreds of thousands of Allied troops was no small feat, and it allowed for the opportunity of a counterattack at some point in the future. The British were able to conserve manpower which would then be redeployed against the German aggressors when the time was right. Without the success at Dunkirk, the chances of retaking continental Europe would be bleaker than ever. But for now, the German advance continued.

While Dunkirk was a victory for the home front, it was soon followed by France's complete collapse. The next offensives after Dunkirk took place at the Somme and Aisne which lay in the path of Paris. By June 14, just one month after the Wehrmacht set foot in France, the French capital had been subdued and occupied by the Nazis.

## American and British Response

Not long after the fall of Paris, the French government had organized terms of surrender to the Germans. Reynaud had resigned and Philippe Pétain was installed as the leader of France. After the Battle of France had come to an end, the northern portion of France as well as the entire Atlantic coastline was taken under direct German control, while the southern portion and the Mediterranean coastline remained in French hands. The new France, however, was a Nazi collaborationist state known as Vichy France, or "The French State." Most of the senior government officials installed by Pétain had advised in favor of aiding and co-operating with Hitler whenever the opportunity arose. The French State even adopted Nazi racial laws and began persecuting Jews without any prodding from Berlin. Some historical accounts blame the pre-war French right-wing for the reality of Vichy France, as many of them had been sympathetic to European fascist causes like those in Italy and Germany. In any case, hostilities had ceased by June 25 of 1940, by which time both Denmark and Norway had also fallen under Nazi occupation. After the Battle of France, Germany had near complete domination of continental Europe, and the Allied powers had been removed from it.

Although British leadership were devastated by how rapidly the proud French nation had disintegrated, the Dunkirk evacuation lent hope to both civilians and the armed forces. In fact, some see Dunkirk as the true beginning of World War II—it was at this point that both the British and Americans began to fear that they might soon be standing alone in the world against fascism and the seemingly ever-expanding Nazi Reich. The British feared that the Americans would never come to their aid, and the Americans feared the British would surrender or perish, leaving Germany free to command the entire continent. The mainland was of course already all but lost, but British leadership, specifically Churchill, were still unwilling to surrender or make peace. Instead, they took a more desperate and bellicose stance. This included the British demand that the French government, still their allies on paper, hand over all of their naval vessels to Britain. When the French refused, they instead requested they sail them to neutral ports so that the Nazis at least could not commandeer them. Even the American Roosevelt administration insisted that the ships be removed from Hitler's reach and assured the government that if they didn't abide, they would be permanently forsaking good relations between their two countries. In the face of French non-cooperation, the British soon launched Operation Catapult to eliminate the chances of Germans seizing the French navy—at Mers-El-Kebir in Algeria, the Royal Air Force (RAF) attacked and sunk a significant portion of the French navy stationed there and firebombed other port areas. It was technically an instance of intentional friendly fire, but it was arguably an important move. Regardless, it soured Franco-British relations.

For the U.S.A., the fall of France was alarming, but it was not enough to bring the nation into the war, or even pull the population out of its isolationist anti-war fervor. It did, however, prompt significant changes in the country's war preparation. Congress took steps to enhance America's combat readiness and boost their wartime production capabilities. Importantly, they passed a bill establishing a larger, "two-ocean" navy for both the Pacific and Atlantic seaboards and made efforts to fully staff the armed forces. Canada and the U.S.A. also joined together in a mutual defense board to invest in the development of military resources and technology. Roosevelt was still unable to convince the nation of the need to take up arms, but the steps taken after the Battle of France were vital to the eventual reclamation of mainland Europe.

The fact that the Allies had lost their foothold on the continent meant that any counteroffensive would inevitably require a naval invasion, setting the stage for the fateful D-Day landings of 1944. This would be made more difficult by the fact that Italy had officially joined the war effort on the side of Germany in early June. Mussolini had initially hoped to postpone open war until 1943 at the very earliest, but Germany's wild success in such a brief period of time prompted him to join up with the Nazis. Had the outcome of the Battle of France been different, it's possible that Italy would not have joined the war at all and might even have joined on the part of the Allies. But Britain's continued rebukes against Italy as well as economic sanctions and the increased British naval presence around Italy already forced Mussolini to take sides. The Battle of France is what solidified their commitment to Germany against the Allies.

## The Battle of Britain

After France had fallen, the next most obvious threat to German expansion was the British. They still possessed a formidable navy and air force, and the Dunkirk evacuation averted a catastrophe for the army. Still, they had just lost their largest ally and were more alone than ever. The world had expected Hitler's sights to be on Britain, but he continued to delay any decisive action against the country until his hand was forced. After all, France's rapid and decisive defeat provided huge momentum for the Nazis, momentum that would be squandered if they idled too long. But it was still not until early July of 1940 that Hitler even considered invading the British Isles. Hope of a truce with Churchill was lost by the time France fell and plans to subdue his country were soon underway. The democratic world, even the anti-interventionist United States, now feared for the war to come.

### Raids on the Coast

Overall, the scope of what became known as the Battle of Britain was not grand. It wasn't the biggest in terms of manpower, armor, destruction, or casualties, but it did have massive implications for the rest of the war. If the Allied powers had faltered yet again and the full weight of the German war machine was allowed to cross the English Channel into Britain, the United States would be the last world power standing in opposition to Nazism. Even if the United States did declare war against the Axis after a hypothetical fall of Britain, any hope of a naval invasion into continental Europe would be seriously hindered without the use of the British Isles as a base of operations. Further, Roosevelt would be faced with a possible two-front oceanic war once the Japanese empire inevitably joined the effort. This was a battle that needed to be won.

*A British WWII-era bomber plane*

A few months after the Dunkirk evacuation, the Luftwaffe began a coastal raiding campaign against British naval and port targets, and also intensified the convoy raids against merchant ships. Initially, the primary targets had been RAF structures, bases, and crafts, in an attempt to cripple Britain's air power. This was a worthy goal, as the coming Battle of Britain would be the first major battle fought entirely in the skies. But why prioritize striking at the RAF over landing troops and moving on toward London? When Operation Sea Lion was conceived, it did indeed call for a large naval invasion into the British homeland, but the most severe impediment to this was the strength of the British Royal Navy.

German naval command had repeatedly insisted to Hitler that an invasion across the channel, and thus the success of Operation Sea Lion, could only be possible if the Royal Navy were distracted elsewhere or significantly cut down in size. Further, the Luftwaffe was required to be able to provide sufficient support for the troops landing on Britain's beaches.

Herman Göring gave assurances to Hitler that the Luftwaffe would be able to guarantee these conditions, but the prerequisite to all of this was gaining unambiguous air superiority over both the English Channel and at least the southern portion of England. This would require the destruction of the RAF. The first phase of the plan consisted of *störangriffe* (in English, "nuisance raids," or "disruptive attacks"), but in July, the attacks intensified. Shipping lanes came under assault as well as airfields near the British coast. Aircraft production facilities, many of which had been built and expanded in the pre-war arms buildup, were also targeted in an effort to disrupt the RAF's supply chain. Although the German air force mounted an intense operation over British skies, they were by this time lagging behind the British in terms of technology. The German "Stuka" dive bombers, which once dominated European skies, were now being outclassed by British fighters whose German fighter counterparts could not keep up with them. Before the end of August 1940, German aircraft losses were nearly triple those of the RAF. It was quickly becoming clear that the Luftwaffe would not be able to keep the promises it had made to clear the skies over Britain to make way for a German landing. Still, the fighting had been intense enough to be a strain on the British, and they would not be able to keep up a prolonged defense indefinitely. Something would have to change.

### The Blitz

Military structures were almost exclusively the Luftwaffe's target in these early weeks, but by the fall of 1940, this would no longer be the case. Soon, Britain's civilians would become the deliberate target of German air raids. At the end of August 1940, a wayward Luftwaffe pilot had traveled off course from his target and accidentally released his bomber payload directly over central London. The news distressed Hitler, who had been hoping to bomb the military into submission, thus forcing a surrender before a bloody and expensive invasion was necessary. Britain's government had, of course, assumed that the attack had deliberately targeted British citizens, and well before Hitler could make his case that the attack was unintentional, Churchill ordered a retaliatory bombing of Berlin. If Hitler was panicked and regretful before, he was now enraged. He ordered more London bombings which began in earnest that September, and they were to continue for months. The first major bombings happened on the 7th and continued for fifty-seven days without break. London was the hardest hit by what in Britain came to be known as "The Blitz," but numerous other British cities were also hit, notably Birmingham, Glasgow, and Belfast.

*A German fighter plane*

At first, the bombings were nearly constant and indiscriminately launched day and night. It was soon realized, though, that the inferior German planes were sitting ducks during daytime operations, and the civilian raids became exclusively nighttime events. Still, the Blitz was brutal and forced the British government to shift much of their wartime focus to developing ways to protect their citizens from a seemingly unending barrage. Maintaining morale on the home front was paramount, as pressure on Churchill from the masses to sign a peace deal is exactly what Hitler was aiming for with the constant bombing and firebombing of populated areas. By the end of the Blitz, countless bombs had been dropped across cities in the British Isles, tens of thousands of British subjects were killed, and millions were left homeless.

While the Blitz was destructive to the home front and civilian life, it was the result of Nazi high command allowing themselves to be distracted by revenge. The mistaken London bombings allowed for the massive shift in the Luftwaffe's focus away from military targets, and thus, allowed the RAF much needed breathing room. Although German aircraft losses were heavy during the Battle of Britain, they were still managing to inflict heavy losses on Britain's limited resources. The success of the battle and the diversion away from air bases allowed the RAF to rebuild, restructure, and prepare for a future offensive. If the Germans had continued on their course, it's possible that the RAF would have been sufficiently incapacitated to actually allow for Operation Sea Lion to be prepped, an undertaking which had been abandoned as a realistic probability well before the battle ended. The success of the Battle of Britain and the survival of British courage through the Blitz allowed for hundreds of thousands of men who escaped Dunkirk to be put to use once more. A Britain that remained in Allied hands would serve as their jumping-off point when they sailed for Normandy four years later.

In total, the Battle of Britain lasted roughly 82 days, from July to October of 1940, and the Blitz began shortly before. However, the so-called Battle of the Atlantic, which consisted of naval and submarine warfare throughout the Atlantic Ocean (over control of British supply lines), would continue for the remainder of the war and was made possible by the fall of France, and German access to the French coast. Ultimately, the Germans gave up on any hope of conquering Britain in the near future, and in the face of unshaken British will, the Blitz ended by May of 1941.

There was finally respite, but the question remained: Why did the Germans so drastically reduce offensive action against the British, their only major enemy at the time? As it turned out, Hitler was not discouraged by the first major upset of his campaign, and instead, set his sights on a new conquest. The Wehrmacht were on the move once again and the Luftwaffe were needed elsewhere.

# CHAPTER 2:
# **OPERATION BARBAROSSA**

When the Luftwaffe air divisions were pulled away from the Atlantic coasts, their new destination would be the far eastern frontier of the Reich. Deciding that Germany needed a major victory after the failure of the campaign against Britain, Hitler chose to forsake the Molotov-Ribbentrop Pact he had signed in the summer of 1939. Soon, German forces would cross the border within Poland that had been established after Hitler and Stalin's joint invasion of the country and enter the Soviet Union. Initially, Hitler and some of his generals had imagined a rapid collapse of the communist government in Russia once the invasion began, but what followed instead was one of the worst German mistakes in the war, one which made the Battle of Britain feel like a resounding military victory by comparison. Operation Barbarossa, as the invasion of Russia came to be known, was a crippling defeat for the Nazis.

## The Winter War

The Soviet-Finnish War in the winter of 1939–1940 was not actually a part of Operation Barbarossa, but it is important in understanding how the invasion of Russia was conceived. It may be surprising that the so-called Winter War is an important part of the overall story, considering it took place outside of the broader World War II alliance system and only consisted of the Soviet Union and Finland as combatants. Indeed, it was a curious war even at the time—barely anyone outside the area knew much of anything about Finland and even less about why the Soviet Union would want to invade them. For one, the two nations had a serious historic rivalry and their respective governments had been at odds for some time. Emerging out of the First World War, Finland had organized itself as a vehemently anti-communist state and for the most part retained a pro-German stance during the interwar years as well as during World War II. Needless to say, public sentiment within Finland was deeply anti-Soviet.

In addition, the Soviets had been aiming to create a puppet state on their northwestern frontier. They feared for the Russian city of Leningrad which lay worryingly close to Soviet borders and wanted to have Finland as a strategic buffer zone. As for why the Winter War is important, there are two main reasons. First, it provided an important training ground for the Soviet Union's Red Army, much the same way Ethiopia provided practice for the Italians, and Spain for the Italians and Germans. Fighting through intensely harsh winter conditions, as they did that winter, gave them valuable experience that they would need before long, after Hitler's betrayal. Of course, the Winter War would end up being disastrous for the Red Army, so it turned out to not be an ideal training or preparation scenario. The fact that it was a debacle for Stalin is perhaps the most important outcome of the war—it convinced Hitler that he should invade the Soviet Union.

## The Battle of Suomussalmi

Prior to the Winter War, but after the successful invasion of Poland, the Soviet Red Army was firmly confident that a potential invasion of Finland would be a painlessly easy undertaking. Soviet manpower eclipsed that of the Finns and the Finnish countryside lay bare and poorly defended. In fact, Soviet high command anticipated the invasion to last only about twelve days before the government in Helsinki capitulated. In the case of Poland, the Russians had relied on the Wehrmacht to subdue the majority of Polish resistance before the Red Army strolled into the country. The Winter War, however, would make them realize exactly how unprepared they were to undertake a large-scale invasion on their own. In addition to their overconfidence and lack of preparedness, the Soviet generals in charge of the coming invasion (notably General Meretskov) were also unaware that they were heading into one of the coldest Finnish winters on record and the Soviet invasion force would be battling through mountainous terrain in absolutely frigid temperatures.

On November 30 of 1939, the invasion of Finland began without an official declaration of war and launched incursions across the Soviet-Finnish border. The invading force consisted of roughly 600,000 Soviet troops (Engle & Paananen, 1992) commanded by General Meretskov, who was in charge of planning and execution. The Finnish government had seen the writing on the wall for some time and were anticipating an invasion. As a result, the defensive strategies of the Finns were seriously underestimated by Meretskov. Despite the fact that Soviet military experience was far more extensive than that of the Finnish army, they were repeatedly outclassed and outmaneuvered. Many Finnish defenders were not soldiers but rural folk, farmers, and hunters. As a result, many of them had been trained to be crackshots since childhood and made for formidable sharpshooters, with some of them achieving legendary status. They were also highly skilled at traversing the countryside by ski, which made them far more mobile than their Soviet counterparts. Engaging in guerrilla warfare almost immediately to counteract the Soviets' traditional warfare, Finnish soldiers were able to dart around on skis and harass Soviet soldiers and patrols before quickly disappearing into the snowy white abyss.

On the day of the invasion, at around 9 a.m. Helsinki time, panic struck the city as air raid sirens went off and the sound of bomber planes could be heard overhead. No bombs fell yet, only pamphlets filled with Soviet propaganda, claiming that the Red Army's intention was not to harm the Finnish people. This proved not to be the case. Possibly as retaliation for not receiving an immediate surrender, by 3 p.m. that afternoon, Soviet planes rained bombs over the capital, killing hundreds of civilians, destroying large portions of the city, and leveling buildings, including schools. The bombings continued and the Finns did their best to combat them with a lack of anti-air capability. Blackout periods, where all lights in a city were turned off in order to confuse pilots on nighttime bombing runs, were used but were basically useless. The city was consumed by flames that could be seen from miles away.

When the Soviets first crossed the border and made advances into Finland, they set up a puppet government based out of the first Finnish town, Terijoki, that they occupied, or "liberated," as Soviet propaganda claimed. Otto Kuusinen, a Finnish communist, was installed to run the so-called Finnish Democratic Republic, the satellite state which the Soviets claimed was the legitimate Finnish government. Stalin had quite a bad habit of creating these puppet states—nominally independent, but in reality, directly controlled by Moscow. Kuusinen was, no doubt, seen as treasonous for taking part in the communist mini-state project, and after the Soviets failed to take the country, he fled to the Soviet Union to avoid persecution in his native Finland. Initially, the Soviets were winning mild successes and making decent progress pushing into the interior. Soon, though, fortunes would change at the Battle of Suomussalmi, a strategically vital part of Finland. Knowing the Red Army was en route to the town, Finnish Colonel Hjalmar Siilasvuo was dispatched to the area. Before Soviet troops had reached the outskirts of the town, Siilasvuo had evacuated and torched the area to deprive the long-marching and overtired Soviet soldiers of any hope of resupply or respite.

The Soviet division charged with taking the area was the 163rd division, who were only meant to secure the town but not actually occupy it, as the area was deemed too difficult to defend from a counterattack. Due to the circumstances, the 163rd occupied the town anyway in hopes that the Soviet 44th division would reach them in time with supplies and relief. Now, the main task at hand for

Siilasvuo was to ensure the 163rd and 44th divisions never met up, thus rendering the 163rd helpless against a Finnish strike. Initially, the Finnish soldiers had retreated from Suomussalmi across the frozen lake behind the town, and the 163rd had continued to attack them from the other side while the Finns bided their time. While this was happening, Siilasvuo's forces continued to harass and stall the 44th. The 163rd were making barely any progress in striking at the Finns and were exhausting their resources in doing so. Eventually, they gave up and decided simply to wait. This presented an opening for a Finnish counterattack on December 11, which was successful. The Soviet occupiers were routed and forced to retreat back across the frozen wastes from where they came, passing by the fields of dead Soviet soldiers who had frozen to death along the way. The retreat from Suomussalmi was almost as disastrous as the defense of it: Days later, lost Soviets were still found wandering the Finnish countryside, with many dying of exposure. Thousands of Soviets had died, and the rest were scattered and some captured.

Now, the Finnish troops at Suomussalmi were free to join Siilasvuo's forces and aid in the destruction of the 44th Soviet division. They were invigorated too, having armed themselves with the equipment left behind by the 163rd in their fevered retreat. The Soviet forces, bogged down by Siilasvuo, had clear air superiority during the battle, but it barely mattered. The fighting here involved such close-quarters combat that any attacks on ground troops would almost certainly kill more Soviets than Finns—all the bombers could do was observe the carnage from above. By the time the Finns from Suomussalmi had arrived, the situation was already grim for the Soviets. Their supplies were now running short, and soldiers were beginning to feel hunger pains. After repeatedly requesting retreat orders from Soviet General Alexei Vinogradov, the troops were finally given permission to abandon their positions by January 6 of 1940, but by then, it was too late. Supplies had long since been depleted, many soldiers had already given up and scattered, and the troops who remained had been fighting on empty stomachs for days in freezing conditions. By the end, most of the 44th lay shot dead or frozen, with over 1,000 more taken as POWs (Engle & Paananen, 1992).

After the Battle of Suomussalmi, the fate of the invasion was all but sealed. It was a hugely important victory for the Finns and contributed the most to the Soviets' inability to subdue the country. It was also an internationally humiliating defeat for the Soviet Union—a supposed "world power" had been bested by a tiny country that most people knew nothing about. The Nazi Reich paid particularly close attention. To their leadership, it was evidence that the Red Army were unprofessional, outdated, backward, underequipped, and lacked any manner of discipline. It was the Winter War that encouraged the Nazis to view the Soviets as weak and unable to make war, and ultimately led to the decision to invade the Soviet Union after the failure of the Battle of Britain. So, Operation Barbarossa, perhaps the most consequential campaign of WWII, would have occurred much later and much differently (if at all) had the invasion of Finland not ended in a resounding Soviet defeat.

**Operation Platinum Fox**

Before addressing the core of Operation Barbarossa, the Second Winter War (also known as the Continuation War) should be briefly addressed. On June 29 of 1941, just days after the initial German invasion of the Soviet Union, German and Finnish forces pushed into the Soviet Union from Finnish territory in a broader campaign called Operation Silver Fox. Operation Platinum Fox refers specifically to the battle over the Soviet port city of Murmansk, a vital port to the Soviet defense effort. Overall, it was a small battle with massive implications for Barbarossa, of which Platinum Fox was one of the first operations. The battle was launched from the Petsamo region of Finland, mostly by the German unit named Army Norway (German forces drawn from Nazi-occupied Norway). The commander in charge of Army Norway was General Paul Nikolaus von Falkenhorst, who oversaw the efforts against Murmansk until the battle ended on September 21.

Initially, the German and Finnish push was successful, but as in the first Winter War, the tables soon turned. This time, it was the advancing Germans who were faced with crippling supply issues, a lack of maps or knowledge of the area's layout and were battling in harsh conditions which the Wehrmacht were not used to. As a result, the German advance quickly slowed to a crawl. Eduard Dietl, the commanding general placed in charge of the Murmansk assault, had repeatedly requested reinforcements and was routinely denied until finally German troops were reassigned from the Balkan area and Norway to Murmansk. Most reinforcements were to arrive via the Arctic waters around Scandinavia, but both British and Soviet naval presence in the area hampered these efforts and critically delayed the landing of support troops. Even when they did land, the arriving troops were untrained for combat in these conditions and offered little help to Army Norway. The disorganization and lack of supplies allowed for a Soviet counteroffensive against the stalled advance.

Although Dietl and other German officers repeatedly insisted that further assaults were impossible, they continued to receive instructions to launch more. By mid-September, Dietl's forces finally retreated, unable to make siege or successful assaults against Murmansk. The Wehrmacht had a new top priority, as the push for Leningrad had begun earlier that month. Murmansk was always considered a secondary objective of low priority anyway, and so the Germans never planned to "die on that hill," so to speak. As it turned out though, their top priorities were to be far more disastrous than Platinum Fox was. It was one of the very few Soviet successes in the early days of Barbarossa and was a foreboding hint to what was to come in later months. And, while Murmansk was not a vital objective for the Germans, it was an important victory for the Russians. Murmansk was a critical base for the Soviet navy and a key port through which mass amounts of military aid and equipment poured into the Soviet Union from the Allied nations. After the U.S. joined the war, just a few months after Platinum Fox, Murmansk's ports saw even heavier traffic as American supplies poured into the USSR. This equipment was key for the coming battles on the Eastern Front, particularly the pivotal Battle of Stalingrad. Before the Wehrmacht marched on Stalin's city though, the Soviet capital of Moscow fell into crisis.

## The Battle of Moscow

Operation Barbarossa was designed and planned so as to deal a rapid and decisive defeat to the Soviet Union and to recover the momentum that was lost with the Battle of Britain. To this end, the Germans sought out important and prestigious targets for their conquests early on. The most important of these early cities was the Soviet capital itself, Moscow. It was the seat of Soviet General Secretary Josef Stalin, and the fall of the city would mean an internal crisis within the Soviet government and the relocation of the Central Committee (the decision-making body of the government). It was believed that Stalin would likely flee before the German army made it to the outskirts of the city, and that conquering Moscow would be no difficult task. In reality, the Battle of Moscow was hardly a "battle" at all. The Wehrmacht were unable to push into the capital and no fighting took place within city limits—a half-hearted siege and a shattered retreat was all they could muster in the end. Moscow was a turning point in the war, but it would not be the last blow to the German war machine on the Eastern Front.

### Defeat at Brest

The first major battle of the early days of Barbarossa took place on June 22 and lasted until June 29 of 1941, the same day Platinum Fox began. It was the first major offensive of Barbarossa, and initially the Wehrmacht had projected that with Luftwaffe support, they would be able to fully capture the Brest fortress as well as the surrounding area on the first day of the assault. The attack happened quickly and took the Soviets by surprise, but that was not enough to secure a rapid victory, and it soon became obvious that this would not be a one-day battle. Still, the German army was able to surround the Brest fortress before long. Many Soviet soldiers were able to escape before complete encirclement, but thousands more were captured. The rest of the defenders stayed at Brest and held out far longer than German command expected, helpfully delaying the initial German advance. The fortress itself was overstaffed with soldiers and officers, which meant that they were dying by the dozens with every artillery shell fired and every bomb dropped. The Soviets still stood and defended Brest for over a week in the face of this continued aerial assault and bombardment.

As it turns out, the fierce defense was purposeful. When the invasion first began, a panicked and surprised Stalin had a meeting with several of his top men, including Field Marshal Zhukov, Vyacheslav Molotov (the cosignatory of the pact with Germany that had been broken merely hours before), and Lavrentiy Beria, the scheming and horrific chief of security and the NKVD. Zhukov was eager to order a counteroffensive, and ultimately, the men agreed to an aggressive, offensive stance. Stalin was hoping for a peaceful end to the war before the Germans were able to push too deep into the Russian heartland. He believed that a strong response to invasion would convey to Hitler that the USSR would not simply roll over and might prompt the Nazi leader to rethink the invasion and seek out a truce. By the time the decision was made, however, it was clearly too late. Unbeknownst to Stalin, the German war machine was conquering territory at a rate of roughly 600 square miles per hour (Pleshakov, 2006).

Ultimately, Brest was a success for the Germans. There were very few Wehrmacht casualties compared with those of the

Red Army, and many were captured as POWs. Strategic bridges, railroads, and transportation infrastructure were seized almost immediately, but it was only repeated aggressive Luftwaffe bombings that forced the Brest defenders into surrender. Civilian morale was also damaged severely, as German occupiers took up sniping positions in buildings and terrorized the city streets. Although the battle ended in a clear Soviet defeat, the manner of the fierce defense foreshadowed Germany's fortunes for the rest of Barbarossa. Brest soon became a powerful symbol of Soviet resilience in the face of attack, and became highly mythologized in post-war Soviet history, much like Dunkirk was for the British. Essentially, both battles were defeats that were taken as victories for the sake of both military and civilian morale.

Another important outcome of Brest was a lesson that both the Germans and Soviets observed. The Wehrmacht was not invincible after all. The legendarily fast conquest of France would simply not be repeated against the USSR, and German ground forces had proven that they were not always up to the task. At Brest, it was only after Göring's air forces stepped up in the face of Wehrmacht failure that led to capture of the fortress. If the Wehrmacht were to have any hope of avoiding a drawn-out war with the Soviets, they would need to perform better. Unfortunately for them, German morale and performance deteriorated in the months following the victory at Brest. For now, though, the Nazis pushed on, well past the demarcation line with which the Soviets and Germans had bisected Poland back in 1939. With Brest conquered and important infrastructure seized, the next major target was obvious, as the road to Moscow now lay open.

## The Push for the Capital

After the German victory at Brest, the Nazis turned their attention to the northeast at the end of summer, toward the capital of Moscow. The march toward the city began in September and by December of 1941, after a treacherous journey, they had reached the gates of Moscow where Joseph Stalin remained. Both the march to and the fight for Moscow ended up being great turning points of the Eastern Front campaign, and indeed, of the entirety of World War II. As Stahel (2015) asserts, "there can be no doubt that Nazi Germany's drive on Moscow was a human calamity with few precedents in history." Still, it was only a prelude to what was one of Nazi Germany's most catastrophic defeats.

By the time German forces had even entered Russian territory proper, they had already won numerous key victories across Poland as well as Belarus and Ukraine, seizing the capitals of Minsk and Kiev, respectively. The struggle within the larger Moscow Oblast area began in earnest in October of 1941, when the war on the Eastern Front had already been terribly destructive and had left millions, soldiers and civilians, dead. If things continued on in this way, Moscow would surely be the next great victory of the Nazi army and possibly the last before the Soviet Union truly collapsed in on itself. In reality though, the city of Moscow falling into German hands had not actually been a realistic possibility for months by this point. The Wehrmacht had exhausted the bulk of its resources, energy, and morale simply *reaching* the city, and they stood no chance of making a strong, spirited push into the city, let alone encircling it completely. A German pullback would have been wise, but ultimately the arrogance of German high command turned Moscow into the disaster that it became.

Field Marshal Georgy Zhukov, who would become a war hero before the end of World War II, evidently never wavered in his belief that Moscow would be successfully defended. According to the plan he devised, the Red Army was to continuously absorb German attacks while retreating eastward toward Moscow. This was meant to allow Germany to overextend itself as much as possible while also forcing them to waste limited resources before eventually staging a counterattack from within Moscow. The fact that the German Army Group Center (AGC), headed by Fedor von Bock, continued to press forward despite a clearly stalled offensive was of great benefit to Zhukov's plan. So, in reality, the fact that the Wehrmacht were within arm's reach of the Soviet capital should not be taken as a sign of success. It was the result of German stubbornness and Soviet planning.

From the outset of Operation Typhoon, as the push for Moscow was dubbed, German morale was strikingly low. By the time they reached Moscow, it had plummeted. Seemingly the only thing that sustained them on the long journey was the desire to take Moscow, but not because that was their mission and not because it was a prestigious military target. Rather, the weary soldiers desperately needed an urban area under their control, in which they could take refuge from the brutal Soviet winter. Many had hoped that if the city could truly be taken in a matter of days, they would soon be receiving fresh reinforcements, allowing some of the veterans to possibly even make it home to their families for Christmas Day. But this was not meant to be, and the ultimate failure of Operation

Typhoon destroyed what remained of the morale and spirit that German soldiers had been holding onto. The winter seemed like it would never end, and meaningful victories seemed helplessly out of reach. The shattered morale at Moscow would have echoing effects for the remainder of the Eastern Front war, specifically on the Battle of Stalingrad

For the majority of October 1941, most of the relevant German armies were hamstrung by severe weather conditions and horribly muddy terrain. The Russian *rasputitsa*, a phenomenon where ice on the Russian plains melts rapidly and creates massive fields of thick mud, had set in and served to bog down all advances. However, when the German advance continued once again, they took note of something interesting among the Soviet defenders. In the earliest stages of the invasion, Soviets tended to operate under a "no retreat" mentality, where soldiers were meant to fight to the last man. This had two effects. First, it was used as propaganda by Nazi Germany, demonstrating that the Soviets had a monstrous view of the world, seeing human life as disposable and forcing soldiers to fight to the death. Second, it allowed for the easy encirclement of Soviet forces by the Germans, which facilitated the complete destruction or capture of all defending units. Because of Zhukov's strategy for Moscow, continuous retreat both denied Germany any significant victories and forced them to continue marching and draining resources. At first, the Wehrmacht took this as a sign of Soviet weakness and waning morale, but it ultimately spelled doom for the invaders. The retreating Soviets, by the time they were ordered to stop retreating and stand their ground at Moscow, would be facing an utterly broken German offensive line.

The German high command also took note of something else, and it was troubling. The Blitzkrieg tactic of rapid deployment and mobile warfare, which had become famous on the Western Front for producing very short battles and massive victories, had become useless in the Russian theater. Here, the Blitzkrieg tactic was dead, never to return. Instead, what followed was a war of attrition where the better-supplied force would ultimately win the day. At the battle of Moscow, that force was clearly the Red Army.

By the time German forces arrived at the city, the Soviet Union alone had access to nearly 30 million tons of oil. Britain and the United States, who had been supplying the Soviet Union, had combined access to over 250 million tons. The German Reich, on the other hand, had less than 10 million tons of oil with which to fuel their war machine (Stahel, 2015). On top of this, the Wehrmacht's AGC was not receiving enough men to replenish their dwindling ranks, whereas the Soviet defenders, who had by this time fully mobilized, were receiving nearly constant reinforcement from the east of the country. One of the main reasons Hitler continued the stubborn advance into Russia was the firm belief that Japan, their ally, would soon invade the USSR from the east, forcing the Soviets to spread their forces thinly over a massive area. This invasion, even by the end of the war, never materialized, and the Soviets were able to funnel troops from all parts of the country to a united front against Germany.

German soldiers were steadily losing any hope of a successful outcome, which was bad enough for the war effort. To make matters worse though, even German officers were starting to lose faith in German high command, and there are reports of some officers openly criticizing the plans of Generals in front of their soldiers, which no doubt caused morale to crater even further. Despite the crisis of morale and the repeatedly stalling offensive, the push continued. When the Typhoon offensive was reluctantly resumed in mid-November, the panzer tank groups of Georg-Hans Reinhardt and Erich Hoepner, north of Moscow, were able to advance with relative success. Heinz Guderian's southern force, though, struggled to organize even a semblance of an effective assault, all the while the Soviet defensive line in front of him was growing by the day. If he remained stalled, hope of encircling the city would be lost. Then, just three days after Typhoon began anew, Guderian sent word to AGC command that all hope of his tank group reaching its target had been lost.

By the beginning of December, two panzer groups (groups 3 and 4) were finally on the verge of reaching Moscow's city limits, but their supplies and morale were long since drained. Without a full encirclement, and without any realistic hope of a successful incursion into the urban zone, the German forces just sat, waited, and observed. Something troubling was happening within the city, though. On December 5, a German soldier named Heinz Fausten took note of the massive numbers of Soviet soldiers amassing within the edges of the city. He recalled: "masses of Russians were suddenly appearing. The sheer number of them left us speechless. . .Where had they all come from?" (Stahel, 2015). Unfortunately for Fausten, the army he saw assembling within Moscow was only the spearhead of the offensive force that Zhukov had organized and sent to launch a counterattack from within the city. Later that same day, Fedor von Bock admitted to high command what had been obvious for well over a month: The offensive was dead, and any delusions of being able to take Moscow must be immediately abandoned.

Without a doubt, defeat at Moscow eclipsed that of the Battle of Britain. One of the main reasons for the launch of Barbarossa was the need to capture Russia's resources and land to offset the effects of the British blockade on the Reich. Therefore, the initial belief that the USSR would collapse in no time was not just a hope. It *had* to happen. But the campaign toward Moscow demanded even more from the failing German economy and it required a massive increase in wartime production. All the while, it was failing to acquire the vital resources it required. To make matters worse, Hitler insisted on the continued systematic extermination of European Jews after the Holocaust began in earnest. Aside from the horrific human tragedy, it further crippled the German economy, as much of it relied on Jewish slave labor. The tide was turning on Germany, but to the Jewish men and women suffering in the ghettos and concentration camps, hope was still bleak.

For the entirety of the push to Moscow, Nazi Generals repeatedly described the battle as a struggle of willpower, where the more determined and hardy opponent would win out. As a result of this, much of the responsibility for the failed siege of the city was put on the soldiers themselves, who were supposedly weak-willed and had embarrassed and let down the German *volk*. Unsurprisingly, it was disastrous for soldier morale. But it also signaled what became a theme in German high command: failure to take responsibility. The refusal to acknowledge higher-up strategic errors allowed these errors to be repeated over and over. This was most consequential at the Battle of Stalingrad, yet another calamity for the German war machine. German strategy suffered a further setback, though. Walter von Brauchitsch, commander-in-chief of the German military during Typhoon, was in poor health and had received the brunt of Hitler's anger after the failed Moscow siege. He was removed from his position and Hitler chose himself to replace Brauchitsch. From now on, Hitler would be the supreme commander of all German forces. Hitler's decision-making skills proved highly questionable though, which was made especially obvious at Stalingrad.

Moscow also happened to be the beginning of the end of the German propaganda industry headed by Joseph Goebbels. Letters from soldiers at the front line had reached home, containing news about the horrible conditions, and this severely damaged morale on the home front. Otto Dietrich, the Press Chief for the Reich, had to begin immediate damage control and insisted that no photographs be taken or published of German soldiers on the Eastern Front unless they were clad in full winter gear. It was an attempt to shield the public from knowing how severely the government had under-equipped their relatives fighting abroad. The damage was done, though, and many Germans already had the feeling that their government was lying to them about the situation in Russia. Worse still, during the Battle for Moscow, something else happened that was dreadfully worrying to German soldiers, generals, civilians, and Hitler himself. They had a brand-new enemy to face. At the end of 1941, the United States threw their full weight across both oceans and took up arms against the Reich.

# CHAPTER 3:
# AMERICA ENTERS THE WAR

Prior to the outbreak of war in Europe, the specter of a different war was looming over the United States. The US had remained firmly isolationist up until the end of 1941 in regard to European affairs, but they still viewed supremacy over the Pacific as their right. In this arena, they had just one major contender—Japan, an Asian archipelago on the other side of the ocean. Japan and the US had been at odds for a long time, dating all the way back to 1853 when US Commodore Matthew Perry sailed to Japan, demanding that the nation open up its ports to international trade, or risk invasion. Since then, Japan had industrialized, modernized, and had created a formidable military apparatus. They had even developed their own conception of a Japanese "master race," similar to Nazi ideology. Japan, at the time led by Emperor Hirohito, viewed the nation as destined to dominate all other Asian peoples and land. This was in direct conflict with America's own ambitions in the region, which included economic domination.

Even without the events of the Second World War, an eventual war in the Pacific likely would have materialized on its own. American and Japanese ambitions seemed irreconcilable, and anti-Japanese prejudice among the American public was staggering (the prejudice had already resulted in the ban of Japanese immigration to the United States in 1924). Then, in 1940, the Axis powers of Germany, Italy, and Japan signed the tripartite pact which guaranteed mutual defense of the members. This meant that the United States, in the event they joined the war, would immediately find itself in a two-front conflict and be forced to split their military power. This too was a serious strain on the trans-Pacific relationship. Ultimately though, it was Japan and Japan alone that shook the US awake, out of its anti-interventionist coma.

## Pearl Harbor

Since 1937, Japan had been at war with China in an attempt to expand their territory from Japanese Manchuria and into the immense Chinese resources. The United States and the West had been firmly against Japan's military actions in the east and had been supplying Chinese resistance with equipment in an attempt to slow Japan's expansion. This was a major frustration to the Japanese Imperial Army (JIA), but more concerning was Japan's frightening lack of access to oil. There was plenty of oil available in the Pacific, namely in the Dutch East Indies, but Japan was denied access to it by the Western nations. The Japanese government had attempted to negotiate peacefully to avoid war, but their demands went unmet. The Japanese war machine was becoming more desperate as 1942 approached, and something drastic would have to be done. This would require waking the American people from their collective isolationist slumber.

## An Isolated America

Isolationist sentiment in America is as old as America itself. From its founding days, even George Washington expressed a desire for the new nation to remain separated from European affairs, and vice versa. It became especially forceful after President James Monroe's so-called "Monroe Doctrine," which argued that America and the European powers occupied two separate spheres, between which military and political interests should not cross. In other words, Europe stays out of America and America stays out of Europe. In the 1930s, though, a new kind of isolationism had formed in America, due to a combination of the economic effects of the Great Depression and the still-fresh memory of World War I. The American public did not want to send a new generation of American men and boys to die in yet another European conflict. By this time, many even believed that it was a mistake to allow President Woodrow Wilson to convince the nation to join the first World War in the first place.

Although Democratic President Franklin D. Roosevelt was very eager to involve America more deeply in international affairs because of Hitler's threatening presence in the 1930s, his efforts were hamstrung by the American Congress which, at the time, was dominated by staunch anti-interventionists. Even after the invasion of Poland and the outbreak of mass war, the US public barely budged from their position. Congress was able to send limited aid and supplies to the Allies in Europe (including, eventually, the

USSR), but remained firm in their rejection of joining the war effort against Hitler in any serious way and were especially against sending troops. Even the publicized human rights violations of the Reich against Jews and other population groups did little to sway public opinion—after all, many of the public were anti-Semitic, anyway, or at least held disregard for the Jews of Europe. Although much of the population was apathetic toward the war, worse were the segments of the American people who were indeed advocates of Nazi ideology. The most notable of these segments were the German American Bund.

## The German American Bund

In 1936 Fritz Julius Kuhn, a German-born, naturalized American, formed the German American Bund, also known simply as "the Bund." It was created with the goal of uniting all Americans of German heritage and founding a national, pan-German movement in support of the fatherland. It was an organization that espoused isolationist sentiments and advocated for friendly relations between the United States and Nazi Germany. In practice though, the Bund sought to attain enough political power in the US to be able to influence foreign policy and to sway public opinion in Germany's favor. They often used smear tactics and conspiratorial accusations against opponents, and had, at several moments, claimed that President Roosevelt's hostile stance toward Germany was the result of him being advised by a secretive cabal of communist Jews. His administration had also supposedly sold out to the godless Soviet Union. The Bund even had a counterpart to Germany's Hitler Youth program, which was a youth program designed to indoctrinate children with the ideologies of Hitler and Nazism. The Bund's version taught children to speak German, salute the swastika, and listen to famous speeches by Hitler.

Although German Americans were a very large ethnic group within the US, the best estimates suggest that the Bund had less than 10,000 members at its peak. They were spread across the nation, claiming membership in all states except Louisiana. They claimed the most influence by far in New York and the Tri-State area, where they owned and operated "camps" in Long Island and New Jersey, named Camp Sigfried and Nordland, respectively. Despite their relatively small membership numbers, much of their rhetoric was still popular with many in America and they often attracted thousands to their rallies. The rise in media attention from their rallies were counterproductive though, as it also revealed the Bund's more extreme, vitriolic, and anti-Semitic policies. Although casual anti-Semitism was rampant in the 1930s, these policies were not popular nationally. Still, as late as February of 1939 a crowd of 20,000 amassed in New York's Madison Square Garden to promote the idea of a Jewish conspiracy within the Roosevelt administration (Bell, 1970).

Clearly, the Bund's goals stretched beyond German–American unity. They were undoubtedly sympathetic to the Nazis and their racial laws and envisioned a future America which would be co-operative, or possibly even subservient to, the greater German Reich. After the invasion of Poland in 1939, the Bund knew it was a potential cause for a declaration of war, and so issued a declaration to the government demanding that the nation remain neutral and not interfere with the ambitions of Nazi Germany.

Indeed, this resonated with many in the country who also did not want the Poland invasion to be a catalyst for mobilization. At the time, the Bund could still try to throw its weight around and make "demands" of the US government, but this would change very quickly in the winter of 1941.

### December 7, 1941

Just off the coast of China and Korea lies the homeland of the Japanese Empire, the principal enemy of the United States. Both polities had ambitions of dominating the Pacific region and each had been making plans in case of a future conflict since at least the 1920s. The US had protested Japan's aggressive expansion, which by the early 1940s was getting extremely expensive for the Empire to maintain, especially in mainland China. Moreover, the Japanese military was starved for oil by this point and desperately needed to secure these raw resources to prevent its war machine from grinding to a halt and leaving the nation vulnerable to American offensive campaigns. The situation was indeed grim—before the end of the fall of 1941, the Japanese Imperial Navy (JIN) alone was consuming nearly 400 tons of oil *every hour* (Coox, 1994). Ultimately, it was decided that if war with the United States was ever going to happen, it needed to happen soon, as the resources of the Empire were dwindling while those of America were growing.

The main prize for the Japanese in the Pacific would have been the Dutch East Indies, the island group in the South Pacific held by the Netherlands. These islands held large oil reserves, enough to power the Japanese military long enough to wage a successful war, if only they could be seized. Unfortunately for the Japanese, many assumed correctly that there would be no way to do this without provoking the US, Great Britain, or both. If, for example, the Japanese fleet moved on the southern islands, it would require leaving the waters of the Japanese home islands undefended. In the case that the US Navy decided to attack, it would be a short and simple affair. If any offensive was to take place in order to seize the oil supply of the Dutch East Indies, the JIN would need a distraction.

To that end, JIN Admiral Yamamoto Isoroku devised a plan to launch simultaneous attacks on numerous targets. The main thrust would be a surprise strike against the American Naval base in Pearl Harbor, Hawaii in order to cripple the American fleet while the JIN took the East Indian islands without interference. This would achieve two goals at once, as Pearl Harbor was already a source of concern for Japanese command—Roosevelt had decided to dock the fleet there rather than on the American west coast, a move which Yamamoto called "tantamount to a dagger pointed at our throat" (quoted in Coox, 1994). On top of Pearl Harbor, the Japanese planned to strike at American bases in the Philippines, Guam, Wake Island, and British bases in Singapore, Hong Kong, and elsewhere. Before it came to this, though, the Japanese government attempted a peaceful resolution once more. They demanded the US end its embargo of the island nation and allow the Japanese access to the South Pacific's vital resources.

Japan sent a delegation to the United States carrying these conditions, but in the end, the order to initiate the attack was given before the American response had been officially given. Originally, it was believed that the Japanese launched the pre-emptive attack because they were already expecting a full American refusal. Now though, it's widely believed that there had been a miscommunication between the delegation and Japanese high command, and that the attack was launched with the mistaken belief that the Americans had issued a refusal. In any case, just before 8:00 a.m. on December 7 of 1941, Japanese aircraft and naval ships set out on their mission to attack Pearl Harbor and decimate the naval fleets docked there. There was massive destruction across the two waves that hit the Hawaiian docks. The US Army lost nearly a hundred of their aircraft stationed at the base that day and the US Navy, whose planes had been parked wingtip-to-wingtip across the airfields, lost over half of theirs. Many American cruisers, battleships, and carriers were damaged or destroyed, and American casualties totaled around 4,500 by the end of the assault (Coox, 1994). The personnel at the base were caught off guard and though they scrambled to organize a defense, they couldn't stop what was coming.

The day after this attack, December 8, 1941, the United States finally entered the Second World War. Americans' former commitment to non-interventionism had been completely shattered and Roosevelt was able to rally the American people around the war effort. At this point, the American people had no choice but to accept the fact that even if they stayed out of the war, the war would come to them soon enough. The plan for Pearl Harbor was already controversial to many Japanese commanders at the time, and in the end, it was Yamamoto who was criticized most sharply for orchestrating the attack that finally united the American people against the Axis powers. In keeping with the Tripartite Pact, Germany and Italy both officially declared war on the US, and the US returned the favor. The attacks also marked the end of the German American Bund, whose central committee voted unanimously to disband in the wake of the attacks, and just days later, the US Treasury department ordered a raid on their headquarters and seized all of their documents.

*A photo of Allied Generals. Eisenhower sits middle front with Omar Bradley to the right of him and George Patton second from the left*

Overall, Pearl Harbor itself was a success for the Japanese, and they were able to deal a heavy blow to the United States' naval capacity, at least temporarily. It was disastrous in the long run, however, as it brought the US into the war along with its massive industrial capacity which dwarfed that of Japan. If it were not for these concerted attacks, the United States very likely would have stayed out of the war for years to come, if they entered at all: "Japanese aggression went far to resolve Roosevelt's problem of how to inflame his people to wartime frenzy" (Coox, 1994). Indeed, the President owed much of his success in this period to the brazen JIN. Of course, the US's entry into the war was also consequential for Germany, as it coincided with the Wehrmacht's stalled offensive against, and eventual defeat in, Moscow.

## The Battle of Midway

The Pearl Harbor attacks did much to hinder the US Navy's ability to operate efficiently in the Pacific, but this advantage did not last. Unless the Japanese were able to somehow deal a deathblow to the Americans at sea, the fortunes of the transoceanic war would soon be reversed. The Japanese had succeeded in securing more oil with which to feed their planes, ships, and tanks, but the involvement of the United States now meant that even more production output would be required, and the Japanese would soon find themselves back exactly where they were and contending with a more powerful foe. Each day, it appeared less and less likely that the Japanese Empire would be able to sustain a prolonged war against both the Americans and the British across the Pacific arena, and incursions into British India would be seriously strained if they were attempted.

### The Aftermath

The Japanese were emboldened by such strong early victories in the campaign and were able to take Singapore, Malaya, and Hong Kong from the British, the Philippines from the Americans, and the Dutch East Indies from the Netherlands. There was also a successful attack on Wake Island, which began at the same time as Pearl Harbor and ended in a full American surrender. Still, the Japanese were not untouchable. In April of 1942, the US carried out an air raid (referred to as the Doolittle raid) against the Japanese capital of Tokyo. The raid served as a wake-up call to the Japanese and signaled that their defenses were not impenetrable and that their enemy was far from defeated and powerless. High command in Tokyo realized that another major blow needed to be dealt against the American Navy before Japanese fleets would be able to operate freely through the Pacific without worrying about attacks against the home front.

Before the Japanese attempted this next major move, they had sights on the southern seas near Australia and New Guinea (later renamed Papua New Guinea just prior to independence), both territories of the British Commonwealth. The Coral Sea, which lies between these two islands, was seen as a strategic zone by the JIN and the way to achieve dominance of this region would be to invade and establish air and naval bases at Port Moresby in New Guinea as well as in the Solomon Islands. By early May though, when the attacks were set to begin, Allied intelligence services had already intercepted Japanese messages and uncovered their plans. Before the first invading forces landed, American air and naval forces were being deployed to counter the Japanese.

From May 3 to 8, American and Japanese carrier-based naval planes traded blows and both sides suffered considerable naval losses. In the end, the Japanese invasions were turned away, but the battle was claimed as a victory for both sides—the Americans successfully defended Port Moresby in New Guinea, but the Japanese had sunk the carrier *Lexington* and severely damaged the *Yorktown* (the Japanese believed they had permanently destroyed it, but the *Yorktown* was destined to see action again). Coral Sea was important, and it set the style and tone for much of the rest of the Pacific campaign. It was the first in a long series of major Japanese defeats and it also marked the beginning of extensive carrier-based warfare. Still, a more consequential battle was still to come just a month later.

### The Six-Month War

After the strategic failure at Coral Sea, the need for a decisive victory against the American Navy was needed even more desperately. To accomplish this, Yamamoto decided that it was necessary to lure out the bulk of the US Navy and decimate it in one aggressive surprise offensive. Yamamoto knew that the best chance they had at drawing out the majority of the US Navy's defenses was to strike as close as possible to American home state shores, but another attack somewhere in the main Hawaiian Islands, such as Pearl Harbor, would be too risky. So, the Midway Atoll to the northwestern extreme of the Hawaiian archipelago, was chosen. "Midway" is quite a fitting name, as the atoll is roughly half-way between Japan and US soil. It was fitting for another reason though: The battle that took place here marked the end of the first phase of the Pacific theater and the beginning of the last phase. Japan's good fortune was soon lost, never to be recovered.

Midway was chosen for a large assault because the Japanese had correctly assumed that the Americans would consider the islands to be vital and would therefore pull out all possible defenses to protect them. The goal of the offensive was to send a small vanguard to begin the assault while concealing the majority of the invading force from American eyes. Then, once the US had committed themselves to the defense of Midway, the JIN would reveal the full force of its fleet, taking the Americans by surprise and utterly destroying the unwitting defenders. This would then force the US Navy into a disastrous position from which they would not be able to recover. It would leave the JIN to run free across the Pacific dealing with only scattered Allied resistance while the US struggled to regain its naval capacity. That was the *plan*. It was not reality.

Several issues hampered the offensive at Midway before it began on the 3rd of June 1942. Among these was the fact that in order for any kind of "surprise" to take place, the JIN needed to space out their naval units considerably farther apart from each other, and separate naval groups were also far from the area of operations. The result was that when the time came for the American response and counteroffensive, the disparate fleets were too far removed to be able to launch any effective support of other units. Even if the Japanese fleets had been close enough to coordinate support, it likely wouldn't have meant much, because the Allies had since made even more progress in decrypting Japanese coded messages. These capabilities had only gotten stronger the more the war dragged on and by the time came to defend Midway, they were sophisticated enough to make a drastic impact. In other words, in the summer of 1942 the Japanese had little hope of taking the Americans completely by surprise anymore.

Almost exactly six months after the attacks on Pearl Harbor, the Battle of Midway began, lasting from the 4th to the 7th of June 1942. Ultimately, it was disastrous for the JIN, even though the American forces, led by Admiral Chester Nimitz, were considerably outnumbered just as they had been at Coral Sea. Nimitz was given charge of all Pacific American naval forces once the US entered the war, and he went on to oversee some of the most crucial American victories. All four of the Japanese carriers present at this battle, which included the *Kaga, Akagi, Hiryu,* and *Soryu,* were destroyed by the US Navy and Air Force. The US, who had only three carriers present at the battle, lost only the USS *Yorktown,* the same carrier that was damaged and subsequently repaired at the Battle of Coral Sea. Hope of invading and occupying the Midway Islands was quickly fading and before long, the JIN was forced to flee the battle or risk utter annihilation. The decision was made to retreat in the hopes that the Japanese Imperial Navy would live to fight another day, but the damage was already done—Japan's naval capabilities had been irreparably damaged. Much like Moscow for the Germans, it was disastrous for morale. The defeat was so terrible that injured veterans returning to the home islands were kept in secretive, isolated hospitals and were barred from seeing their families in the hopes that it would contain the full extent of the loss at Midway.

Due to the crippling of the Japanese Imperial Navy and Air Force, the battles in the aftermath of Midway were also largely failures for the Empire. Indeed, Midway "can be considered the beginning of the end of the Japanese Navy," and from this point forward, the Japanese would not win a single major victory against the United States for the remainder of the war in the Pacific (Bongers & Torres, 2020). So, although the defeat itself was terrible for the Japanese war effort, its true significance was that it allowed for the JIN to be continuously hamstrung in subsequent battles, until it was eventually annihilated for good. Some attribute Japan's defeat here to "victory disease," a name for the supposed overconfidence that came with Japan's six months of nearly uninterrupted victories and advances. This apparently allowed them to commit mistakes at Midway, severely overestimating their own ability while underestimating that of the Americans. Some accounts suggest that actually, the Midway battle was essentially a toss-up, and American victory was the result of their better fortunes.

Japanese air capabilities also suffered massively as a result of Midway. Plenty of the Navy's planes were lost along with the carriers that transported them, but the losses went beyond material. The loss of experience at Midway was also considerable—the Japanese tended to keep their best ace pilots in front-line fighting roles so that they could continue to use their expertise in the skies. Indeed, the Japanese had many skilled pilots that rivaled their American counterparts, but the downside to this strategy was that when they lost, they lost hard. In the fighting, the Japanese had lost some of their most senior and experienced airmen which resulted in an overall deterioration in the quality of Japan's pilots. The men lost had to be rapidly replaced which meant an abbreviated training period was necessary, leading to even further erosion to the number of quality airmen. The US, on the other hand, avoided these issues by frequently rotating pilots and promptly promoting airmen that showed promise to leadership positions where they could pass on their knowledge to other pilots, rather than continue to deploy them on active missions and risk losing their expertise forever.

The Japanese would feel the effects of Midway until their final surrender and occupation in 1945. Later battles, such as those at the Solomon and Gilbert Islands in 1943, the Marshalls and Philippines in 1944, and Iwo Jima in 1945, were doomed from the beginning because of the destruction at Midway. Chester Nimitz remained at the helm for all of these battles.

But the larger Axis war plans also suffered. The joint German–Japanese strategy to converge on British India from the east and west before joining forces in the middle had to be abandoned due to the crisis in the Pacific. Resources and equipment needed to be pulled from the continental Asian theater and diverted to the Pacific in order to prevent the US from steamrolling their way to Tokyo and the home islands. Finally, perhaps the most significant result of Midway was that, for the remainder of the war, American air supremacy was all but guaranteed due to the loss of four Japanese carriers. This ensured that by the six-month mark of the Pacific theater's opening, the fate of the Japanese Empire was already sealed.

# CHAPTER 4:
# **STALINGRAD**

Shortly after the American victory at Midway in the Pacific, a new major confrontation was beginning on the Eastern Front. And just as Midway was the ultimate turning point in the Pacific theater, this new battle permanently reversed the direction of progress in the Russian theater. The setting was the city of Stalingrad, where the efforts of the Soviet Red Army were able to steal victory from what was, at one point, almost certain defeat. The German march to the city was destructive enough, just as the march to Moscow had been, but the situation that Wehrmacht troops faced within the city dwarfed that of any previous German catastrophe. It was without a doubt the greatest defeat that the Nazi German Reich had suffered up to this point, and it marked the end of the German advance and the beginning of Field Marshal Georgy Zhukov's push out of the Russian interior and into the German heartland.

## Stalin's City

Stalingrad's name translates literally to the city (or "settlement") of Stalin. It has been known by several names in its history and was originally known as Tsaritsyn when it was founded in the sixteenth century. Joseph Stalin of course renamed it in his honor after he took control of the Soviet Union in 1924 after the death of Vladimir Lenin. After Stalin's death, the new Soviet leader Nikita Khrushchev renamed the city to Volga, then Volgograd, in an effort to remove the image of Stalin and his decades-long reign of terror from the Soviet people's collective memory. In 1942, though, it was still very much Stalin's city. It remains a large urban center situated on Russia's Volga River and during the war, it was a vital industrial hub for the Soviet Union's economy. Both its population and industrial capacity made it an obviously important war goal priority for the Nazi Reich. Securing the city of Stalingrad was apparently important to the German government for another reason, though.

Once the possibility of seizing Stalingrad was put on the table, Hitler became personally obsessed with it. Yes, it would be a boon to the German efforts on the Eastern Front to be able to occupy a large urban city and provide a way station and layover area for German troops to gain much needed respite during the cold months. But Hitler was also chasing a highly symbolic victory. In a way, the struggle to wrest Stalingrad from Stalin's control was envisioned as a struggle between the men themselves, Hitler and Stalin. This was almost certainly due to the fact that the city bore Stalin's name, but it was still a powerful metaphor for the battle between the two dictators and for the ideological battle between German fascism and Soviet communism. Perhaps, Hitler thought, a resounding victory and the subsequent occupation of Stalin's own city would finally cause the Soviet Union to collapse.

As we will see though, the struggle for Stalingrad produced the exact opposite effect. It was another brutal disaster for the Wehrmacht and in many ways, it was the "nail in the coffin" of Operation Barbarossa and of any hopes of subduing the Eastern communists. After the city of Stalingrad was finally rid of the threat of the German army, there would be nothing left to stand in Zhukov's way. It would be only a matter of time before the Red Army crossed back over the Bug River that divided German and Russian Polish territory. Soon, they would be knocking on Hitler's door.

## Another Winter Disaster

As discussed in chapter 2, the failed Soviet invasion of neighboring Finland in the Scandinavia region caused many German military leaders to conclude that the Red Army was a "wholly archaic and demoralized military machine destined for the boneyard" (Clairmont, 2003). Although the disastrous siege of Moscow shattered this illusion for many, German high command would continue to underestimate the Soviets for the duration of the offensive. Hitler, in particular, remained overly confident about their next major targets and apparently refused to learn anything of value from the Moscow siege. But Army Group South, tasked with the bulk of the next major offensive, was not in as bad a shape as the Army Group Center that failed at Moscow, so perhaps some chance of success might not have been doomed after all.

The codename for the Nazi offensive planned for the summer of 1942 was *Fall Blau*, or Case Blue. Originally, it called only for a push toward the Soviet Caucasus region to capture the rich oil fields there in order to maintain the German war machine. The severe discrepancy in oil reserves between the Axis and Allies needed to be remedied if Germany was to avert a military crisis. It goes without saying that these oil fields were an obvious priority for the Wehrmacht, but there were two major problems that complicated the mission. First, the German armies had still been advancing too slowly to meet deadlines from high command. Case Blue was originally intended to get underway in May of 1942 in order to exploit the advantageous summer weather. Due to the long delays in troops advancing into position, the operation had to be repeatedly pushed back. Then, in July of that year, Hitler issued Directive 45, an amendment to the original plan for Case Blue. The directive called for Army Group South to split into two separate armies on their way to the Caucasus region. One group was meant to continue marching to the original objective while the second group was to be diverted and march directly toward Stalingrad to siege and occupy the city, an important industry center for the Soviets. Certainly, Hitler wanted to seize the city in order to create a defensive position to protect the Romanian oil fields, but he also desperately needed a propaganda victory, and there would be none greater than stealing Stalin's city out from under him.

When the directive was issued, it was Hermann Hoth's 4th Panzer Army and Friedrich Paulus' 6th Army that were rerouted to Stalingrad. The commanders of these armies knew that the majority of the weight of this operation would rest on them alone and that reinforcements, if they received any, would be limited. The Moscow disaster had permanently shattered the myth of the "invincible" German Wehrmacht and by February of 1942, a large proportion of the Reich's manpower was eliminated in the retreat from the outskirts of the capital. Still, Hitler had huge ambitions and vicious plans for their next target and its population. His orders were plainly stated by German high command: "the führer [Hitler] orders that on entry into the city of Stalingrad, the entire male population should be liquidated, since Stalingrad, with its thoroughly communist population of a million, is particularly dangerous," (quoted in Clairmont, 2003). Much of Stalingrad, thankfully, had been evacuated well before the Wehrmacht penetrated the city limits.

The delay in the launch of Case Blue apparently did not worry Hitler too much, as he once again expected the city to fall in no time. At worst, he thought, it would be in German hands by the end of summer 1942. The push to the city did not appear completely unwinnable at first. Paulus and the 6th were able to push to the Don River outside of Stalingrad where the Battle of Kalach began on July 25 of 1942. The Soviets had created a bridgehead (a fortified defensive position placed across a bridge in order to prevent river crossings) over the Don to cut off the German advance into the city. But by the 11th of August, the Germans had dispelled the Soviet defenders, secured the bridgehead, and gained control over the passage over the Don. The pathway to Stalingrad was now laid open for Paulus' 6th Army.

Soon, Paulus was able to occupy the surrounding suburbs and then in early September was able to push into the city proper. Just as in Moscow, though, German blitzkrieg tactics proved useless within the urban center of Stalingrad. Instead, there was intense, close-quarters urban combat and guerilla tactics. The German troops were making slow yet consistent progress, but Hitler's vision of the city falling before summer's end did not bear fruit. By October of 1942 though, the Wehrmacht had succeeded in occupying roughly 80% of Stalingrad after fighting through the streets and taking territory inch by inch (Baird, 1969). Despite the progress made by the Germans, the Red Army continued their stubborn defense of the city until such time came that they could launch a counterattack from the small portion of Stalingrad that remained in their hands. As a result of this unwillingness to surrender, German victory continued to be delayed indefinitely.

The unwillingness of the Soviets to surrender dismayed both the German command and soldiers in the offensive. The official newspaper of the *Schutzstaffel* (better known as the infamous *SS*), *Das Schwarze Korps*, published near the end of October that if the Americans or British were the ones defending the city of Stalingrad instead, the battle would've been over in a mere few days. The Soviets, on the other hand, were compared to inhuman beasts whose utter disregard for human life rendered them incapable of realizing when struggle was futile. Stalin was apparently a monster that was willing to spill the blood of every Soviet soldier rather than surrender to the Reich. In reality though, it would be the German high command that showed a reckless contempt for the wellbeing of their soldiers.

Just like the Moscow campaign, the push within Stalingrad had stalled by mid-October of 1942. The offensive was dragging on and Press Chief Otto Dietrich was called upon once again to do damage control. In order to avoid a public relations disaster akin to Moscow, Dietrich was instructed to disallow the publication of anything deemed too optimistic in regard to Stalingrad. Hitler could not risk raising the German public's hopes too high, only to have them dashed violently once again. Ultimately though, Hitler was still inappropriately optimistic about the eventual "eternal" defeat of the Soviets and their communist economic system. Special news editions reporting a grand victory at Stalingrad were prepared on Hitler's orders and were placed on standby to be immediately released upon the long-awaited news of Soviet surrender and evacuation from the city.

This surrender was appearing less likely by the hour, as the stalled offensive lines in the city had begun suffering repeated and sustained Soviet surprise attacks and counterattacks, not to mention the sporadic sniper fire from raised positions in burned-out and half destroyed urban buildings. The Germans attempted to hold their positions against these attacks, but meanwhile, Stalin, Zhukov, and Chief of the General Staff Aleksandr Vasilevsky were busy devising one of the greatest military counter offensives in history.

## Operation Uranus

For several weeks prior to the counter offensive, Zhukov had been biding his time and mustering massive numbers of troops for a fresh, coordinated assault on the Wehrmacht forces occupying Stalingrad. This assault was codenamed Operation Uranus by Soviet command. German forces in the city had, of course, been expecting a counterattack, but they could not have anticipated the size and scale of what Zhukov was preparing. After a long and difficult siege of Stalingrad, the Soviet Field Marshal finally launched Operation Uranus on November 19, descending upon the city and surrounding area in a massive pincer formation. The Red Army began by repeatedly bombarding the positions of the already beleaguered German troops for several hours before moving to divide the German forces and to cut both supply lines and communication between the groups. Uranus' pincer move proved highly effective in relieving the city, and in just three days, Zhukov had completely encircled General Paulus' 6th Army within Stalingrad. They had also already driven out the armies of Germany's allies, including the Italians and Romanians.

Such was the dire position of Wehrmacht forces within Stalingrad, completely cut off from support and supplies. German officers had already been requesting a retreat order from military brass for some time prior to Operation Uranus, and after encirclement, they requested permission to surrender, but all of these were continuously denied. Instead, Adolf Hitler, as the commander-in-chief of all German forces, insisted that Paulus' men remain in the city to defend and hold their positions. The Luftwaffe would then provide the much-needed relief and supplies via airdrops over their positions. Given the number of German soldiers within the city, the amount of supplies, food, and water needed to sustain them far exceeded the capacity of the Luftwaffe. Hitler demanded that Göring deliver to Paulus by air daily an amount that was already a fraction of what was actually needed, but even this reduced amount was too much for Göring's airmen to handle. Even if the Luftwaffe managed to increase their daily payload capacity, it would make little difference as Soviet production was massively outpacing that of Germany by this point.

THE GREATEST BATTLES OF WORLD WAR II

So, the 6th Army were sitting ducks inside the city as the Soviets encroached upon them. In early January of 1943, Zhukov's forces extended terms of surrender to the trapped German soldiers, with the promise of swift destruction in the case of a refusal. Still, Hitler refused to give his blessing and Paulus obeyed. The terms of surrender were denied and two days later, the Soviet assault resumed. The attacks that ensued were brutal, yet Paulus and the 6th held out longer than expected, given their material condition. By the end of the month, though, they could no longer take the pressure from the Soviet assault. On January 22, General Paulus could no longer deny the futility of fighting. He sent a telegram to Hitler advising him that, in his opinion, any hope of a counter offensive against Zhukov was lost.

Before January was over, the German army inside Stalingrad had been split into two separate groups by the Soviet offensive advance. The divided units, incapable of supporting each other or sharing equipment, were more vulnerable now than ever before. The southern pocket of the German forces was still commanded directly by Paulus, who had been separated from the group to the north. It was Paulus' southern pocket that was first to surrender on the last day of January 1943, after the army had suffered a devastating attack by the Red Army, and Paulus had apparently given up on his steadfast obedience to Hitler. If there was no surrender, and Hitler's orders were followed, nearly every single soldier in Stalingrad under Paulus' command would have been destroyed by advancing Soviet troops who, as we will see later on in the Red Army advance, were eager for revenge against the Germans who had attempted to destroy and subdue their Russian motherland. The German forces to the north held out slightly longer, but ultimately laid down their arms on February 2nd and were taken as POWs along with their commander.

The decision to surrender saved many lives from needless death, as the battle was lost regardless, and the fate of Stalingrad was assured. Still, it was an outrage to Hitler, who apparently had fully expected Paulus to commit suicide after he failed to seize the city. This is, apparently, because on the same day as the surrender, Hitler had decided to promote Paulus to the rank of Field Marshal, and German Field Marshals simply did not become POWs. His decision to surrender was seen as weak and as a disgrace to the German nation. Rather than a propaganda victory, Hitler got to experience the deep humiliation of having a high-ranking Field Marshal surrender and be taken prisoner. Paulus apparently did not take kindly to the sleight against him from Hitler and German high command. This, combined with the fact that Paulus had by this point lost faith in the German commanders' ability to make war, led him to become a fierce advocate against the Nazi Reich during his time as a prisoner of the Russians.

Much of the result of both Stalingrad and the siege of Moscow had to do with the difference in equipment and technology between the Red Army and the Wehrmacht. As was the nature of the Soviet Union's slow-to-start wartime economy and mobilization, it took quite some time for their production and manpower to meet the challenge of the Germans. However, once the wheels began to turn, Soviet capability soon vastly outpaced the Reich's. Meanwhile, the German economy was exhausting itself with its continuous wars of conquest, and by the time Soviet wartime production and innovation was accelerating, Germany's was waning. The Soviets rapidly developed new technologies to deploy on the battlefield, while Nazi technology stagnated due to the nation's economic woes. German commanders were aware of this troubling state of affairs and remarked upon it in the aftermath. Heinz Guderian, for example, said "we had nothing compared to the T-34 tanks, to the Sturmovik dive bomber, the Katyusha rockets and their submachine guns" (Clairmont, 2003). Under these conditions, it was almost impossible for the German army to maintain a superior sense of morale during the fighting.

By the end of the battle, over 130,000 Axis soldiers were killed (including some Romanians), nearly 100,000 more were taken as prisoners, and of those, barely 5,000 would ever make it home to Germany (Baird, 1969). Within a month, over half of the captured Germans died while in Soviet captivity, whether from continued exposure, starvation, or prior wounds that went unattended. Stalingrad was without a doubt the worst German defeat of the entire war. The utterly demoralized German army had lost all hope of attaining any significant progress in their advance into the USSR. This was the most significant turning point of the entire Eastern Front campaign, and Stalingrad marked the beginning of the Soviet march toward Berlin. The German forces were scrambling to pull back from Zhukov's offensive and now, the Red Army would soon be marching past Stalingrad toward the west, and there would be no more retreats.

## The Propaganda Machine

Yet another disaster on the Eastern Front with Stalingrad crushed what remained of the Wehrmacht's eastern momentum. The morale of the German soldiers plunged even further from its lowest ebb after the defeat at Moscow. The men in Stalingrad had watched their friends and fellow soldiers starve and freeze to death for weeks after having been seemingly abandoned by the very men who sent them to the city in the first place, and the hurried retreat from the area left even more Germans dead on the frozen Russian soil. Morale on the front line never recovered after the Stalingrad failure, but another crisis of morale on the home front would make matters infinitely worse, as many were quickly losing faith in Hitler's promise of a German Reich to endure for a thousand years. If news of yet another catastrophic loss in the aftermath of Moscow were to break in Germany, internal troubles would be sure to follow closely behind. With a crumbling line to the east, a stalemate stare-down to the west, and mounting losses in North Africa, this would have been an intolerable situation.

The German propaganda machine, headed by veteran Nazi party official Joseph Goebbels, was the tool with which the Reich promoted successes while diverting from failures. In the early phase of the Second World War, it was concerned almost exclusively with the former of these tasks. Since the tables had begun to turn during Operation Barbarossa, this was no longer the case. Goebbels' propagandists and Otto Dietrich's censors were instead tasked with controlling the flow of information about these terrible defeats and ensuring that the sentiments of the soldiers on the ground did not resonate back home in Germany.

When both the Moscow and Stalingrad campaigns began, though, the foolish optimism of the Nazi high command was on clear display, as daily reporting on the great progress of the ground troops was encouraged.

For months, there was nearly constant coverage in Germany of events regarding Stalingrad, and the German public had been eagerly following the developments in what was shaping up to be a significant victory. However, once the tables had begun to turn, the offensive stalled, and troops began suffering Soviet counterattacks within the city, the manner of reporting on the home front abruptly began to shift. Suddenly, news of the Stalingrad siege was scant, and what was instead being reported on was the continued successful occupation of France and the small, scattered victories of German U-boats (*unterseebooten*, the name for German submarine vessels) against the British in the Atlantic. Hitler, it seems, refused to accept another blow to his prestigious ego (as well as to the prestige of the Wehrmacht which had been earned in the first two years of the war). He could not suffer this loss nor the psychological effect it would have on the German people. So, it was decided that it was best to divert attention from Stalingrad, but that strategy was less than effective. Germans at home already knew something was wrong, as many had become accustomed to following developments in the offensive daily and were suddenly being kept in the dark. Simply put, the German masses would have been agitated in any case.

Once General Paulus' 6th Army began to be steadily annihilated, Hitler chose to cease all communication of the events within the city. As the Moscow debacle demonstrated, though, this wouldn't be nearly enough. When soldiers fear death is when they write the most letters home, and the German soldiers encircled by the Red Army in Stalingrad were certainly fearing death. The letters sent from the soldiers of the 6th Army would give their loved ones back home all of the information that the Reich had been keeping from them, and the soldiers' pessimism would almost certainly seep through the letters and into the German public's collective thoughts. This had to be avoided, and so it was ordered that *all letters from Stalingrad* were to be intercepted and confiscated before making their way home. Of course, Hitler and his advisors were correct in their estimation—letters from Stalingrad communicated an irreparable lack of faith in the goals and strategy of the Nazi government. In an analysis of letters sent from soldiers, merely 2.1% were deemed to communicate positive feelings about German leadership. A whopping 60% were considered negative or actively opposed to German leadership (Schneider & Gullans, 1961).

One letter from Stalingrad was especially morose and pessimistic about the campaign and even life itself: "Around me everything is collapsing, a whole army is dying, day and night are on fire. . .the [Soviets] would never show such a lack of understanding for its men. I should have liked to count the stars for another few decades, but nothing will ever come of it now, I suppose." Another soldier questioned the entire purpose of the battle and hinted at his fellow soldiers' lack of faith: "there is no more summer, but only winter, and there is no future, at least not for me. . .They tell us that our struggle is for Germany. But there are only a few here who believe that this meaningless sacrifice could be of use to our country." One letter called out Hitler's failings by name: "We are entirely alone, without help from the outside. Hitler has left us in the lurch. If the airfield is still in our possession, this letter may still get out. Our position is to the north of the city. The men in my battery have some inkling of it, too, but they don't know it as clearly as I do. So this is what the end looks like." Likely fearing what the Soviets would do to the German POWs, he continued, "No, we shall not go into captivity." Of course, there were not many alternatives for these soldiers besides going into captivity, as another Stalingrad letter succinctly points out: "Of course, I have tried everything to escape from this trap, but there are only two ways left: to heaven or Siberia." (Schneider & Gullans, 1961). He was of course referring to death or internment in a Siberian Soviet work camp. Clearly, Hitler was right in his estimation of troop morale, and the Reich had good reason to attempt to prevent these letters from reaching loved ones back home. The German censorship apparatus was not perfect, though, and many of these letters ended up reaching their targets.

In addition to the interception of soldiers' homebound letters, Hitler advised Martin Bormann, the head of the Nazi Party Chancellery, to aggressively suppress any pessimistic sentiment on the home front, as well as to stamp out any behavior that could be considered treasonous (i.e., loss of faith in Adolf Hitler as leader of the German Reich). Eventually though, this facade crumbled, and Hitler was forced to allow the Stalingrad situation to be explained. After all, several of his advisors, by this point, had disagreed with the plan to continue to cover up the Stalingrad failure. Rumors were circulating widely throughout Germany, with some claiming a defeat that was actually worse than reality, which caused more panic than was necessary. The death of the highly touted Stalingrad offensive was clear for all Germans to see, and so there was not much more to gain by keeping the public out of the loop. Still, Hitler attempted to conceal certain facts. For one, the German public simply could not find out that the troops within Stalingrad had surrendered. Nor could they know that Friedrich Paulus, a newly appointed German Field Marshal, had repeatedly asked for a surrender order and had directly defied Hitler's orders to continue fighting. Instead, the German public were told that Paulus' 6th Army fought valiantly to the very last man, unwilling to surrender to the beast-like communists. The accounts of over 20 German generals also surrendering were disconcerting as well.

The attempt to conceal the nature of the German defeat was foiled too, however. This time, it was due to a Soviet fear strategy. After Stalingrad, the Soviets had begun periodically broadcasting over German airwaves and announcing the names of German soldiers who had been taken as prisoners of war after their humiliating surrender at Stalingrad. Finally, Germans at home were receiving actual news of their family and friends who had been sent to fight in Russia. Citizens had been captivated for days by the broadcasts, listening eagerly for news, whether good or bad, about their loved ones. The Soviets even began sending postcards (both real and fabricated) directly to the families of some of the POWs. With this, the Soviets had shattered the illusion of Stalingrad for the Germans and ruined Hitler's plan to preserve the honor and prestige of the Wehrmacht, as well as his own. Still, Paulus' 6th Army was heavily mythologized by the Reich as valiant martyrs who willingly gave their lives in defense of the fatherland from the forces of savage Bolshevism.

The ultimate failure of Stalingrad led many Germans, both servicemen and high-ranking officials, to lose faith in Hitler as the supreme commander of Axis forces. His decision-making ability was obviously easily clouded, and he could not be trusted to remain on task. But as we've seen, Hitler's reputation was not the only casualty of the aftermath of Stalingrad. The German propaganda machine, which had attempted at every turn to cover up the truth of the failed offensives of Operation Barbarossa, had lost the trust and faith of German military men and civilians alike. The people understood well enough the purposes of a propaganda apparatus, but the intentional confiscation of their letters, most of which would be the last communications from the soldiers to their families, was a step too far. German propaganda, as well as Hitler himself, was now being viewed with contempt and distrust. The legacy of the defeat at Stalingrad was also long lasting. In future defeats, such as in Tunisia in the spring of 1943, the German press was prohibited from making any reference to, or drawing any comparisons with, any aspect of the 1942–43 winter campaign, specifically the Battle of Stalingrad.

Men, material, territory, and trust. These were the sacrifices of Stalingrad. The Wehrmacht was decimated, Russian ground was being rapidly retaken, German command was in question, and the faltering German economy was further deprived of resources. Most significantly, the loss at Stalingrad meant that the precious eastern oil fields which Hitler had hoped to capture and defend were now doomed to fall into the hands of the enemy, never to be recovered. The German war machine, already stuttering and smoking, would now be even more poorly supplied in the battles that were to come. Stalingrad was, without a doubt, the most severe material and psychological defeat that Germany suffered in the Second World War, and it was only the beginning of the reversal of Germany's outward expansion.

# CHAPTER 5:
# **ACROSS THE**
# **MEDITERRANEAN**

In the grand scheme of the Second World War, the battles that occurred across the Mediterranean from Europe, in North Africa, appear to be mere sideshows next to events in Russia or the Pacific. Consequential battles were occurring across the world, so why pay attention to a few scattered units scrambling about in the desert, in places few in Europe had ever heard of? Indeed, the battles that took place in the North African theater were not the largest, neither in terms of scale nor casualties. None of the battles were as decisive as Stalingrad or as sensational as Pearl Harbor, and the outcome of the war was certainly not to be determined in Libya or Egypt or Tunisia. Still, the fight for control over the British, French, and Italian colonies along the southern Mediterranean coast were important in understanding the overall outcome of the war, and the decisive desert victories were key to the outcome of the North African theater which had ripple effects on the war effort in Europe.

## The Battles at El-Alamein

North Africa during World War Two was divided up by the European powers. To the far east, Britain controlled Egypt. Between Egypt and Algeria was Italian-controlled Libya, and (Vichy) France controlled the rest of western North Africa, including Algeria and the important Atlantic and Mediterranean ports of Morocco. When Mussolini first forced his Italian nation and its people into Hitler and Churchill's war, the Battle of France was already too far along (and long since decided) for the Italians to accomplish much of note. But the southern portion of France was not the only border they shared with their new enemies. Initially without the aid of their Nazi friends in Germany, the Italians decided to take the battle to the arid and coastal deserts across the sea. Naturally, they had their sights set on the prize of British-occupied Egypt, complete with vital access to resources and key travel ways. It also contained the fabled Egyptian city of Alexandria, founded by the Macedonian conqueror Alexander the Great. It was important to Mussolini for a different reason though: it was one of the major cities of the Roman Empire at its height. For Mussolini, who wanted to reform as much of the former Roman borders as he could, it would have been a prestigious victory. And so, it was decided: A new theater opened in North Africa in 1940.

### Italian Invasion and Operation Compass

When the Italian forces initially crossed over from Italian Libya to the east into Egypt, they intended on marching across the Egyptian coastal territory until eventually reaching and capturing the prized Suez Canal. The Canal was an important strategic goal, as it connected the Mediterranean to the Red Sea (a thin sea separating north-eastern Africa from the Arab gulf) and provided the quickest and most convenient sea route between British waters and their colonies in India, also known as the British Raj. Controlling the Suez Canal and the vital Port Said, Britain risked being cut off from the much-needed supplies from their Indian territories. In reality though, the British Navy was a formidable force with which the Italians could not hope to contend, even with the occasional aid from German U-boats. In any case, a supply crisis was the last thing the British needed, and the Suez Canal would have been a terrible strategic loss, as would the loss of the port in Alexandria and the capital of Cairo.

Luckily for the British though, the Italian invasion was doomed from quite early on. The Italians had more than enough men present on the continent to launch an effective and prolonged foray into British Egypt, but they would be doing so with a critical lack of motorized vehicles, including troop transports and tanks. This meant that for the duration of the campaign, the Italians would be able to achieve absolutely no tactical or strategic maneuvers with any speed. Worse than that, infantry units would be forced to march on foot under the brutal heat of the North African sun in the parched coastal deserts. Units without transport support were limited to a daily advance of 30 kilometers at maximum (Sadkovich, 1989). The invasion quickly developed into a slog and eventually the Suez Canal, which lay toward the eastern extreme of Egypt, was given up as an unrealistic goal.

Very soon after the initial declaration of war, on June 14, British forces from Egypt seized the Italian Fort Capuzzo in Libya, near the border. After the British halted their advance, the Italians were able to recapture Fort Capuzzo by the beginning of July, repel British counterattacks, and begin their push into Egypt in mid-September of 1940. The advance was predictably stalled after a mere few days, though. They had already suffered numerous delays and before they were able to take any significant strategic targets, their ground troops, already exhausted and under-supplied, were forced to pause and await reinforcements and fresh equipment. In lieu of continuing the advance, the Italian forces instead built fortifications along their front line to hold the position against inevitable British counterattacks. The Italians had just made it past Sidi Barrani, an Egyptian town they were able to seize from Allied forces.

By the time the Italian advance was forced to halt, it was already clear that they would be at a severe disadvantage when it came to resupplying their armies. The British had clear naval superiority over the Italians which, when combined with the air support the RAF was able to provide, made it so that the Italian home fleet could scarcely even defend their ports in North Africa. Lacking equipment, weapons, effective transportation and even water, the Italian troops' morale in the North African colonies soon plummeted. Much like their German counterparts during the upcoming campaign against Soviet Russia, Italian troops in Egypt and Libya were beginning to question the capabilities of their commanders and the logic of their plans. As a result, the performance and willpower of Italian troops in the upcoming battles would be severely diminished. This was compounded by the ongoing issues with motorized equipment for the ground infantry. By November of 1940, the Italians had less than 4,000 vehicles present to support the roughly 100,000 Italian soldiers in Cyrenaica, the eastern portion of Libya (Sadkovich, 1989).

Under these conditions, the Italians, even with their fortifications, were vulnerable to a major counterattack. Indeed, in early December the British launched their first significant offensive in the region, under the codename Operation Compass. Initially, Operation Compass was meant to be an assault against the five fortified positions the Italians had erected around Sidi Barrani, but British success was so rapid that their forces continued to push well into late winter of 1941. Very quickly and without much effort, the Italian forces were fully pushed out of Egypt and were retreating across the Libyan coast. They incurred heavy losses during the operation: Within just two days of the successful assault and advance, tens of thousands of Italian troops had been captured as POWs. At the time, it looked probable that the coming months would witness a complete collapse of Mussolini's North African forces.

This initial Italian invasion, as well as Compass, were key in opening up offensive theaters in the eastern, and later western portions of North Africa. The dire situation that the Italians were left in also had ramifications for Hitler's efforts on the continent. He deemed it necessary to prop up his Italian ally, and decided to send large numbers of troops, as well as German General Erwin Rommel (who commanded the 7th armored division during the Battle of France), to support the war effort in the region. This move spread the German continental forces thinner just for the purpose of averting a complete Italian defeat. Rommel was (and is) a highly mythologized figure in German military history. He is

101

generally considered to be a strategic genius for his efforts in France and North Africa, but others believe that his accomplishments and skills were purposely exaggerated. Regardless, here is where he would earn his nickname, the "Desert Fox."

Operation Barbarossa and the subsequent push for Moscow would begin later that year, only exacerbating the problem of Germany's overstretched manpower. Having to take Rommel away from the European theater as well as an entire Army Corps (the so-called Afrika Korps) was perhaps not worth prolonging the demise of the Italians in Libya. The Italians, for their part, had failed to secure important oil reserves across British North Africa and the Middle East, but the quickly deteriorating defensive position meant that they would soon also be losing whatever oil reserves they held themselves in Italian Libya, further crippling Italy's wartime capability. The arrival of Rommel's Afrika Korps was certainly a boon, but their success would not last.

**The First Battle**

Under Rommel's command, the performance of Axis troops vastly improved in Libya. Soon, the rejuvenated Italians with their German reinforcements were able to push the British back through Cyrenaica and into Egypt once again, forcing the Allies back on the defensive. In the coming months, they would be reaching the Egyptian town of El-Alamein and its surrounding area, where the decisive First and Second Battle of El-Alamein would take place. As a side note, the titles of these battles are not quite fully descriptive, as they comprised numerous small operations in and around the region that were sometimes connected to the main battles, and sometimes not. Referring to the overall operation as the "Battle of El-Alamein" is useful nonetheless, and mostly a result of historians attempting to make chronological sense of the chaos that happened during the months of the battles.

As the combined German and Italian forces pushed their advance in an effort to remove the British from Libya, they were already beginning to fear fresh supply issues. As they pushed, their main supply line from the Libyan capital of Tripoli was being stretched thin. The Axis forces hoped to quickly capture the Libyan city of Tobruk near the Egyptian border in order to form a new base for Axis supply lines. This would provide a vital forward base for the continued push into British Egypt. Unfortunately for Rommel, attempts to seize the city failed, and starving out the defenders was unlikely, as the besieged Allied troops inside were being continuously resupplied by the Royal Navy, which neither the Italians nor the Germans could do anything to stop. Still, without establishing a supply base any closer to Egypt than Tripoli, Rommel continued his eastward march.

Despite these issues, by July of 1942 the Axis forces were deep into Egyptian territory and were based near El-Alamein, a town less than 70 miles from the famous and coveted port city of Alexandria, as well as other key Mediterranean ports. In June, British forces were sent on the retreat after the Battle of Gazala near the border and less than three weeks later, British forces had been encircled at Mersa Matruh, resulting in a devastating defeat and the capture of thousands of Allied soldiers. Mersa Matruh was also a terrible disaster for morale, and after Rommel had begun speeding his forces toward El-Alamein (and well beyond, as was assumed at the time), many in both the Allies and Axis believed that Alexandria and Cairo would inevitably be in the grips of the Italians and Germans before long. Mussolini was especially confident that the total capitulation of Allied forces in Egypt was imminent. Indeed, Rommel's forces were advancing quickly, but they were also shorthanded and exhausted, by this point. And as it turned out, Mersa Matruh was not intended to be the site of any British last stand anyway—British General Claude Auchinleck had wanted to pull back to El-Alamein before losses became too severe, as it would be a much more easily-defended area. He was correct.

Axis forces were preparing for a decisive attack and swift breakthrough at El-Alamein, followed by a spirited march across the coast and down toward the capital of Cairo on the Nile River, headquarters of the Allied forces within Egypt. Axis movement began on the first of July, but within days, the advance was stalled yet again, and Rommel's forces were put on the defensive, a rare occurrence for Rommel since having taken charge of the forces in Libya. Desperate to avoid losing ground and being pushed back once again into Italian colonial territory, Rommel's forces stood their ground and were forced to repel numerous British attacks while also struggling with nearly constant harassment from the RAF as well as attempted disruption of their already vulnerable supply and communication lines. By the time this first set of battles and skirmishes were over in late July 1942, neither side had achieved a decisive victory. The First Battle of El-Alamein was essentially a stalemate—both sides inflicted considerable losses. The British were at least able to prevent the Axis forces from advancing further into the interior toward Cairo and the Suez Canal. The morale victory was significant for the Allies, who had been looking for a win to offset any pessimism on the home front, but the more important victory was still to come.

## The Second Battle

Once the first series of battles at El-Alamein were concluded, the commander of the Allied defenders, General Auchinleck (as well as others), understood that the German position would be untenable for much longer without a better supply line to relieve the troops. Meanwhile, the British position would become more and more secure the longer they were able to keep Axis forces at bay. For this reason, a fresh German offensive was expected sooner rather than later, as prolonging the standoff was not in their favor. But Auchinleck was also being pestered by British high command (including Churchill himself) to begin a large offensive against the German positions. As it turned out, the Allies, including the United States, were planning a large invasion of Axis territory in North Africa and Churchill was fixated on winning a decisive victory before the invading troops made footfall later in 1942. But Auchinleck knew his troops were still weary from the first series at El-Alamein, and so, delayed an assault as long as he could. The punishment for this was severe. In August of 1942, Winston Churchill and Alan Brooke, Chief of the Imperial General Staff, took off for Cairo to reprimand and relieve Auchinleck from his command position. His intended replacement was killed before being able to take up his full duties in North Africa, and so the responsibility eventually fell to Bernard Montgomery, a now famous British military leader.

*Field Marshal Montgomery observing the battlefield*

In early September, fortunes seemed to change after the recent British victory at Alam El Halfa, just outside of El-Alamein. Once again, the Germans were placed on the defensive in the tug-of-war that didn't seem to be going anywhere. In the meantime, though, British forces were being constantly resupplied while their counterparts in the German Afrika Korps and the Italian X Corps were both suffering. The demand for resupply of German (and Italian and Romanian) forces in the Eastern Front campaign, which had begun to seriously turn against the Germans, rendered Rommel's desert forces a distant priority. Italian high command was also stingy in what they sent to the North African theater, and what they were willing to send was often intercepted and destroyed by the Royal Navy. In comparison, Britain and her allies were more than happy to send all they could: "America and the Commonwealth gave Britain whole-hearted support" (Sadkovich, 1989). Indeed, if it was to become a war of attrition, Britain and the Allied forces would be the clear victors.

After the Battle of Stalingrad began in earnest in August of 1942, Rommel was holding out hope for a rapid German victory to allow some of the Axis forces committed to the Eastern Front to move southward and aid in the taking of Egypt. Hypothetically, some could have been shipped to Rommel's forces in the west of Egypt, while others could have moved down the Levant and assaulted Egypt from the east. This would never come to pass though, and Rommel's dreams of a quick and easy Stalingrad campaign, as we've seen, would never be realized. They would remain undersupplied until the inevitable British counterattack, which was coming quickly with Montgomery at the helm. British high command began immediately pressuring the newly appointed Montgomery to launch the attack that Auchinleck had continuously postponed, but he was able to take the time to fully rearm and plan a thorough attack. The result was Operation Lightfoot, designed to carve paths through the German minefields scattered across the open deserts ahead of their positions so British tanks would be able to pierce through their defensive lines.

On October 23, shortly after Rommel had been sent back to Germany due to illness, the British caught the Axis forces by surprise with the sudden launch of Lightfoot. At the time, the British forces led by Montgomery had mustered nearly twice as many infantry units as the Germans, now being led by Rommel's second-in-command. The assault was preceded by a confusion campaign designed to fool the Axis as to the location and time of the offensive, which German and Italian command had been anticipating. The British first experienced trouble with the official launch of the Second Battle of El-Alamein, with several Allied convoys being sunk, and the German minefields (consisting of hundreds of thousands of explosive devices) taking much longer to destroy or disarm than expected. Still, Axis casualties were severe and the fuel problems they had been experiencing were only exacerbated by the defensive. The Luftwaffe was also of little help to Axis ground troops, as was the Italian air force. This was opposed to the RAF, which ensured ground support for Allied forces for the duration of the operation.

In the end, superior equipment and better supply access won the day, and the German forces were routed before mid-November of 1942. Forces of the Afrika Korps and X Corps were aggressively pursued across the Libyan desert and coastline, losing tens of thousands of soldiers in the process, either left behind as corpses or POWs. They first retreated to, and took up defensive positions at El Agheila, a Libyan coastal city in west Cyrenaica, but were quickly forced to retreat further across Italian colonial territory. Finally, the British were awarded a clear and decisive victory, rather than the anticlimactic first set of battles at El-Alamein. And unlike Dunkirk or the Battle of Britain, this victory did not come with an asterisk—it was an unambiguous and thorough victory. The impact on morale was important, despite it taking place in a "secondary" theater of the war. Combined with the introduction of the Americans to the Allied cause, British morale was at a peak.

The defeat at El-Alamein also put Axis hopes of taking the Suez Canal, and thus of restricting mobility between Britain and her Indian colonies, out of reach. It was a key tactical victory—the British were forced to learn how to rapidly, efficiently disable mass quantities of anti-tank and anti-personnel mines and to quickly maneuver in mine-laden terrain. Further, the degree of defeat at El-Alamein caused a rift in German-Italian relations. German high command often blamed the disaster in North Africa on the Italians' weak will and inability to fight and criticized their generals' ability to lead. As it turned out, the battle did essentially mark the end of Fascist Italy's ability to fight meaningfully. In the battles that followed as a result, the majority of their armored and motorized units would be annihilated. For these reasons and more, the defeat at El-Alamein was significant and marked the beginning of the end for the Axis in North Africa. And Operation Torch was soon to be the nail in their coffin.

## Operation Torch

With the Axis on the retreat in North Africa, no hope of invading Britain to the west, a crumbling front line in Russia to the east, and with the United States committing itself to the war effort, the stage was now set for a large Allied offensive, at long last. The Axis defeat at El-Alamein was significant, but German and Italian presence in North Africa remained and so long as it did, it posed a threat to Allied consolidation of the region and its resources. Ultimately, the British desired to close the North

African theater once and for all before taking the fight to the heart of the Reich in mainland Europe. The operation that was to follow, along with Stalingrad, fully dispelled any notion of German military dominance, and Erwin Rommel's reputation would suffer particularly severely as a result. Hitler and Rommel's personal relationship also became severely strained, and the German Field Marshal, in turn, began losing faith in Hitler's ability to lead and command military forces. The tensions between the two would bubble to the surface in dramatic fashion two years later. But Hitler and Rommel's relationship wasn't the only one to suffer as a result of the campaign in North Africa, nor was the Italo-German relationship. The leaders of Vichy France, Germany's puppet state and the polity in charge of much of Axis-held North Africa, also fell out of favor with the Germans in the wake of what was known as Operation Torch, a massive strike into Axis territory on the Mediterranean coast.

### Anglo-American Co-operation

After the United States entered the war, they operated independently in the Pacific against the Japanese for roughly a year. By the end of 1942 though, they and their British allies were finally ready for their first large joint operation in the Atlantic theater. The only problem was where to strike first. There were many options, including coastal France, northern Europe (i.e., directly into Germany), German-held territory in Scandinavia, North Africa, Greece, or Italy. Churchill and the British were firmly insistent that North Africa should be the site of the first co-operative strike with their new wartime ally. It was their desire to wipe out all Axis presence on the northern coast of the continent and close the North African theater.

It would have been a great victory for morale (both for civilians and soldiers, as many servicemen would finally be able to retire from the oppressive desert heat), and the British would be able to more easily shift focus and strength back onto mainland Europe. The Americans, on the other hand, were desperate for a direct naval invasion into France or northern Europe in order to more swiftly apply pressure to the German heartland. The reasoning for this was sound: The Americans understood that the Soviets were perhaps the best bet that the Allies had of winning the war, and they desperately needed relief. So, an Allied strike into mainland Europe would force Hitler to divert troops back across Europe to meet the western advance, thus allowing the Soviets to more easily steamroll their way out of Russia and into the Reich. The British justification also made sense. If Europe was targeted while North Africa remained a contested area, their potential landing zones would be limited, and Germany would be fully expecting France, the Low Countries, or Germany itself as the target. Once North Africa was in Allied hands, however, it would be anyone's guess where they would strike next. Southern France, Italy, and the Balkans were all opened up as potential invasion routes due to Operation Torch.

American Generals were mostly unified in their opposition to prioritizing North Africa, but Churchill was implacable. If things were to progress smoothly, it would have to be his way for now. So, President Franklin D. Roosevelt gave his blessing and approval to Operation Torch, under the condition that the operation be launched as quickly as possible so as to clear the way for a European invasion. In general, the plan was to invade the French North African colonies of Morocco and Algeria, at the time occupied by the Vichy regime. Three primary strategic targets were to be taken first: the famous (thanks to Ingrid Bergman and Humphrey Bogart) port of Casablanca in Morocco, as well as Oran and Algiers in Algeria. This plan too was a compromise. Most American Generals wanted landings confined to the Casablanca area in Morocco, but the British were eager to land closer to Tunisia in order to press Rommel's forces from the west. The British plan involved passing massive military armaments through the Strait of Gibraltar if invasions were to be made in Algeria, and this had to be done delicately and with tact. If not, the Allies risked arousing the anger of Francisco Franco, the fascist dictator of Spain who happened to be ideologically aligned with both Hitler and Mussolini. Spain was in enough trouble of its own, but there was genuine fear that a large operation in Spain's backyard could draw a new enemy into the fold. The revised Operation Torch still went ahead, though, and Spain never took part in the conflict.

After originally planning the assault for some time in October of 1942, it was given the greenlight in early November. On the 8th, a force consisting of somewhere in the neighborhood of 60,000 to 80,000 British and American troops began making their preliminary naval assaults and beach landings. The invading force at Casablanca, in the far west of the region, took the city and port within a few days. The Oran assault was easier—many of the defenders in the city surrendered after only a naval barrage courtesy of the British Royal Navy.

Algiers was perhaps the simplest task, though. Prior to Operation Torch's launch, leaders from the Allied forces had been having clandestine meetings with certain French officials who the Allied intelligence community believed might be willing to turn against Nazi Germany and the Vichy French collaborators. It was, of course, assumed that in the aftermath of Torch's predicted success, the Allies would need capable French leaders to retake control of the colonies. The French Resistance (which was led by the famous Charles de Gaulle) defied the collaborationism of Philippe Pétain after France fell in 1940 and was already undertaking their own operations both in France and their colonies, including North Africa. By the time the Allied invading force landed in Algiers, the Resistance had already staged a successful coup and arrested several Vichy France collaborationist leaders. There was still Axis resistance to the Allied advances, but much of the heavy lifting had been accomplished prior to Torch's success.

### The Closing of the North African Theater

After the Allies had succeeded in capturing the key ports in Morocco and Algeria, the landing forces began pushing the Axis defenders from the west, toward Tunisia and its capital, Tunis. Due to the disastrous Axis campaign at El-Alamein, Rommel's forces were also being pushed toward Tunisia from Egypt and Libya from the east. Soon, the last remnants of the Afrika Korps and the X Corps would be sandwiched, trapped on both sides by the advancing troops of Bernard Montgomery and Dwight Eisenhower, the American General put in charge of the forces of Operation Torch. Rommel had seen the writing on the wall for some time and had attempted on several occasions to convince Hitler that North Africa was a lost cause and that he needed to pull out the remaining forces to be redirected elsewhere immediately. Unfortunately for Rommel, who had begun to fall out of favor with Hitler, he was instead ridiculed and derided for his concern and apparent display of weakness.

To Rommel's dismay, he was ordered to press on in the pointless defense in Tunisia. His eventual defeat was both inevitable and highly predictable. On May 13 of 1943, shortly after the Nazi's had lost Tunis and as Rommel's forces were severely outnumbered and suffering supply shortages that were worse than ever before, the Axis forces of North Africa surrendered to the Allies, who took hundreds of thousands of prisoners of war. The loss of North Africa had significant consequences for Hitler and the war effort. Nearly 300,000 of their men, who could have been redeployed to the Eastern Front or to the defense of the French coastline, were now in Allied captivity. Italy's military was also decimated in the desert campaigns, and would struggle to launch any effective operations, offensive or defensive, for the duration of World War Two. Mussolini and the nation were also at their most vulnerable— the Italian mainland as well as their currently-held territory in southern Europe (the Balkans) now lay open to further Allied invasion, using North Africa as a launching point. This, in fact, did happen, and the success of Operation Torch paved the way for the future invasion and capture of Sicily, as well as total Italian surrender later in 1943.

Obviously, a massive morale crisis for the German public soon followed. Still reeling from the utter destruction of German soldiers at Stalingrad, surrendering an entire theater of battle was a sign to many at home that the German war machine (which had run roughshod through one of Europe's premiere militarized nations a mere three years earlier) was now out of steam. The Germans now needed to consolidate their military, knowing that their enemies would not be resting on their laurels for a moment. The Russian campaign was looking grim, and naval incursions into mainland Europe by the Anglo-American bloc seemed like they could begin at any moment. On the Allied side, though, the immediate issue was solidifying their occupation of North Africa. As part of the pre-invasion negotiations regarding the Vichy French military's role in the aftermath of Torch, French Admiral Francois Darlan was chosen as their man. Darlan, admittedly a Nazi collaborator, was able to keep his position after Axis surrender in exchange for a guarantee that Vichy France's military would remain co-operative in North Africa.

Seen as a betrayal by Hitler, Darlan's switching sides led to the collapse of German-Vichy French relations, and even prompted Hitler to invade southern France (the portion not directly annexed by the Reich) to stamp out pro-Allied sentiment on the continent. It was perhaps the right move, but this resulted in the Wehrmacht's manpower being even more thinly spread than before. In any case, Germany had lost one of her allies and would soon be losing another. Besides nations, Hitler was also losing key men. Operation Torch and the subsequent German surrender had caused a rift in Hitler's relationship with Erwin Rommel, one of his top Generals and advisors. An enraged Hitler believed Rommel had shown true cowardice and incompetency, while Rommel had begun losing faith in Hitler's vision. Eventually, Rommel would go on to betray Hitler in an attempted coup, for which he was punished by being forced to commit suicide. The breakdown of Hitler's trust in Rommel was a worrying sign, and Hitler soon began lashing out at many of his top military leaders.

Despite the fact that many consider the campaign in North Africa to be largely inconsequential, it's indisputable that Allied victory in Morocco, Algeria, Tunisia, Libya, and Egypt allowed the eventual invasions of mainland Europe to progress more smoothly and discreetly than would have otherwise been the case. Further, the Allied forces were able to secure the vital oil reserves in North Africa and the Middle East and prevent the Reich from being able to gain fresh fuel for their panzer tanks, motorized divisions, and Luftwaffe fighters and bombers. Without oil, the German panzers didn't run, and without the panzers, the backbone of the entire German military structure was handicapped. Perhaps most significantly, the Axis was denied access to and occupation of the Egyptian Suez Canal in As Suways, the most important strategic canal in the world at this point. German and Italian dreams of driving a sword between Britain and her colonies in India would forever remain a dream, as the British Royal Navy ensured. No, the North African theater was not a sideshow.

# CHAPTER 6:
# **THE MANY ROADS TO BERLIN**

The outcomes of the most significant battles described above had, by 1943, left the German Reich in a precarious position. The disastrous failures at both Stalingrad and Moscow had irreparably doomed the dreams of German eastward expansion and as a result, the German concept of lebensraum (and the Italian *spazio vitale*) was tossed in the waste basket of history. If Germany was to acquire more living space for its land-hungry population, it was clear that it would no longer come at the expense of the Soviet people. The Wehrmacht were now being pushed from the east back toward the German heartland. After the decisive Allied victory in Operation Torch in North Africa, the Axis forces were now also retreating back to their territory from the south and the Italian peninsula was now exposed and vulnerable to further Allied invasions originating from the African coast. On top of all this was the anticipation of another massive invasion from the west. No longer were the Allied forces waiting around hoping for a miracle and desperately trying to hold off the ruthless German advance. Now, they were more ambitious, emboldened by repeated victories. They now had their sights set on Berlin, the seat of Adolf Hitler, the man who plunged the world into a war that dwarfed even the First World War, the greatest conflict mankind had ever known. And by 1944, Axis fears of a coastal invasion of France came true. From the east, west, and south, Allied forces were now pressing toward central Europe, converging on the Nazi capital.

## The Battle of Kursk

In 1943, the Axis faced two pivotal moments that represented their last chances to prevent further Allied advances from the east and south. Hopes of devouring Russia swiftly had long since died, but it was perhaps still possible to halt their retreat and preserve some of their previous land gains. To the south, Germany's Italian allies were in a dire position and had already earned the contempt of Hitler and the German leadership. Even the most famous Nazi General could not prevent the utter collapse of the Italian armed forces. By the summer, the last chance of an Italian victory came and passed, and Germany, who had just lost Vichy France as a war puppet, would lose yet another European ally. Kursk in Russia and Sicily in southern Italy were the final chapters of their respective theaters and they created the conditions by which Germany would, by 1945, be sandwiched and surrounded on all sides by Soviets, Brits, Americans, Indians, Canadians, Australians, and more. Germany was up against the world without even a wall to put their backs against.

## Operation Citadel

After the Red Army dealt the Wehrmacht a staggering defeat at Stalingrad and captured just shy of 100,000 prisoners of war, they were marching west with a renewed sense of morale and fierce love for their Russian nation (indeed, the Soviet mentality of protecting the motherland bordered on the pathological). By the beginning of 1943, a gap had been created within the German defensive line which allowed the Red Army to pierce through and successfully recapture the city of Kursk on the Moscow-Rostov railway in the Kursk Oblast region of Russia in early February. Soon after though, the Soviet advance had stalled and the Red Army led by Georgy Zhukov were left with a bulge in their front line, based around the recaptured city of Kursk. A bulge is also known as a salient—it is a protrusion in a military's front line which is surrounded on three sides by enemy territory. They are considered highly vulnerable and prone to rapid entrapment. The defenders at Kursk likely would not have been able to withstand an immediate and prolonged assault, however, the Wehrmacht needed to delay any assaults. Attacking before the end of spring while the Russian *rasputitsa* was still in full force likely would have doomed any large armored assaults on Kursk before they even began.

The codename for the eventual planned attack on the Kursk region was Operation Citadel and it was originally planned to commence as soon as possible after spring. Unfortunately for Nazi General Erich von Manstein, the offensive force once again suffered numerous delays. The present forces were, by this point, severely undermanned and in desperate need of resupply, so a mass assault would need to wait. It was also clear that, due to the lack of available infantry (scant reinforcements were on their way but an insignificant number would be able to make it in time for an effective attack), Operation Citadel would almost certainly have to be undertaken mostly by tanks and armored units. This prediction was accurate—the battle at Kursk ended up being the largest majority tank battle in the history of warfare up to that point, as well as one of the largest air battles in history (though less famous than the Battle of Britain). According to Roman Toeppel, it was actually the largest battle ever, *period* (Toeppel, 2018). Although the preferred metrics for determining the "size" of a battle vary from person to person, Kursk was certainly a monumental battle both in terms of physical destruction, personnel participation, and in the significance of its outcome.

By the time May came around, both Walter Model and Erich von Manstein had grown wary of the plan and were personally opposed to it. In their minds, the assault was likely doomed either way. Attacking during the *rasputitsa* would severely hinder the movement of their panzers, which the Wehrmacht would be forced to rely upon. But if they waited for it to end, it would only allow the Soviets to build even more significant defenses. The Soviets knew an attack would likely happen on the vulnerable Kursk, and they also knew that German armor would have to do the heavy lifting, which would give them a significant advantage if the assault was delayed too long, and they were given time to adequately prepare. Model and von Manstein were not confident in the Wehrmacht's ability to overcome these challenges once the operation was finally ready to begin. Still, it was repeatedly postponed in order to wait for fresh equipment and supplies.

Soon after the bulge at Kursk had formed, the Soviets were originally planning on attacking various targets pre-emptively before the Germans had a chance to counter. But thanks to Soviet espionage and spies in both Britain and Switzerland, the Red Army was able to learn of German offensive plans well in advance of their operation. Though Stalin was keen to continue dealing blows to the beleaguered German army, Zhukov had advised against it and instead recommended that the Red Army first stage a strong and brutal defense in order to weaken the Germans before launching a counter offensive. This course of action was accepted, and Zhukov was given permission to begin amassing huge numbers of both soldiers and civilians around Kursk in order to rapidly construct and deploy defenses. Importantly, one of the main defensive tools used by the Soviets in the Kursk defensive were anti-tank mines. Knowing that the Wehrmacht would be throwing every piece of armor they had into the assault, the Soviets focused on protections against panzer tanks rather than German infantry.

At long last, the German assault was launched on July 5 of 1943. German tanks indeed formed the cornerstone of the Wehrmacht's attack strategy, just as the Soviets predicted. The Red Army inflicted considerable losses from the German armor, but Zhukov had fortunately ordered the main defense force to withdraw from the bulge in order to avoid a swift and decisive defeat of his troops. As a result, much of the damage inflicted upon the German tanks was not done by Soviet tanks or infantrymen, but rather the extensive anti-tank minefields that had been laid along the frontier of the bulge and well into its interior. The Germans began suffering the loss of many of their panzers almost immediately after the assault started, and their numbers were decimated before long. German panzers had already proven that they were well past their glory days of spearheading massive blitzkrieg assaults and securing Axis victories almost single-handedly. Kursk was a deathblow to their armored corps which were already stumbling and struggling to muster anything resembling an effective offensive.

The forces of Model and von Manstein, while able to inflict damage to the defenses at Kursk, were unable to push deeply into the salient before having to halt the advance. Their large pincer movement pressed from the north and south, but the southern forces were barely able to make it 30 miles into the interior. The northern forces fared even worse, barely accomplishing anything and losing large numbers of their tanks. By the 12th of July, the German advance came to a complete stop and in that time, Zhukov and the Red Army had mustered another massive force of armor and infantry. They were ready for a counterattack, which was launched that day.

In the face of this counter, it was only a day later that Hitler officially called off Operation Citadel before the Wehrmacht were able to accomplish a single one of their strategic goals. Hitler's decision to halt the offensive was partially due to the news of a brand-new invasion launched just days before, on July 9. Just as the Axis anticipated, it was an invasion in the southern portion of Europe against Germany's Italian allies. This will be addressed shortly. Some historians doubt that this new invasion was a main cause for the abandonment of Citadel, but it was almost certainly a consideration.

On July 14, the German forces to the south of the Kursk bulge once again tried to reignite the German advance and to entrap Soviet forces in the region in another large pincer formation. Codenamed Operation Roland, the fresh offensive only took one day to stall, as the Soviet forces had successfully pushed through German lines and out of their vulnerable positions before the two arms of the German pincers could even link. Roland was aborted by July 17, again without accomplishing any strategic or tactical victories.

After Roland was forsaken, the troops involved were transferred elsewhere. Most were sent to other parts of the Eastern Front, but some were needed southward in the defense of the Italian peninsula. Zhukov's forces then kept pushing, still taking heavy losses, until they finally reached the Ukrainian city of Kharkov (Ukraine at the time was a Soviet Socialist Republic, or SSR, a semi-independent polity which existed as a state under the broader Soviet Union) on August 12. Kharkov was first occupied by German forces in October of 1941, and on August 23 of 1943, they were completely expelled by the Soviet liberating army.

The German offensive at the Kursk bulge was now officially dead, and the German Reich's armored capability suffered a massive blow as a result of the battle. Their panzer divisions on the Eastern Front were destroyed by Soviet defenses and minefields which the Nazis were unprepared for. Even though Toeppel (2018) argues that the German panzer armies were still, in theory, capable of carrying out offensive strikes even though they had been severely staggered, it didn't turn out to matter much. The Battle of Kursk marked the last time that the German army was able to launch a single significant offensive on the Eastern Front. If Stalingrad was the catalyst for the overall German retreat from Russia, Kursk was the nail in the coffin of the entire German incursion into the Soviet Union that began in the summer of 1941. The German Reich had permanently surrendered any chance of gaining the upper hand while on their trek out of the USSR. Overall, the result of the offensive at Kursk was not necessarily decisive. Even if the Wehrmacht had succeeded in securing their strategic objectives, it almost certainly would have amounted to a temporary delay in the Red Army's overall push toward Germany. The victory was significant in that it allowed Zhukov and his forces to progress toward Berlin at the speed that they did.

### The Landings on Sicily

After the destruction of all Axis presence on the North African coast as a result of the battles at El-Alamein as well as the successful Operation Torch, the possibility of an Allied invasion of mainland Italy was tempting. The nearest point of the nation was less than 300 kilometers from the city of Tunis and the mainland peninsula itself was just slightly further. At the beginning of 1943, the Allies met in Morocco at the Casablanca Conference to determine the next step of their joint offensive—a suitable, logical sequel to Operation Torch. Opinions between the British and Americans differed, but British leadership was able to convince the rest of the Allies that an invasion of Italy should take precedence before any other Mediterranean targets (such as Greece), in order to loosen naval restrictions in the Mediterranean Sea. The Italian navy did not pose much of a threat to the combined force of the British

Royal and American navies anyway, but the elimination of Italian seafaring capacity would allow for complete Allied dominance of the region. It was decided that Italy would be the next Allied target.

Operation Husky was the codename for the plan to land Allied amphibious divisions in Sicily, off the coast of southern Italy, in order to eliminate all land, air, and sea capability from the island before advancing onto the mainland. The landings and subsequent capture of Sicily were facilitated by the conquest of North Africa, and it was from these coasts that the invasion was launched. Malta, an island south of Sicily and even closer to the North African coastline, surrendered by the Italians to the British with barely any resistance and was used simultaneously as a departure point for the invasion and the headquarters for the broader operation. The invasion was set to commence on July 9, at the same time Axis forces were battling at the Kursk salient. American, British, and Canadian forces landed at different parts of the island and began their march toward the Messina Strait, a narrow strip of sea that separates Sicily from the mainland. The Allied forces had succeeded in tricking the Axis forces into believing that the British and Americans had chosen Greece as their next target after North Africa. Because of this, the landings on Sicily went far more smoothly than otherwise would have been the case, and the invading force caught the defenders both off-guard and demoralized.

On July 10, landings were successfully made by the Americans on the southern coast of Sicily, led by General George Patton and his U.S. 7th Army, and by Commonwealth forces nearby on Sicily's southeastern coast, led by British Field Marshal Montgomery and the British 8th. The initial invasion was demoralizing to the already pessimistic Italian troops, as well as Italian civilians. This was especially due to the presence of American forces. In decades prior, the United States had seen massive immigration from Italy, and especially from Sicily. This meant that, with near certainty, there would be relatives, whether close or distant, fighting against each other on opposite sides. This led to a genuine hesitance to fight, as there were many young American G.I.'s who were the sons of Sicilian-born U.S. immigrants. The Italian military had suffered such significant losses by this point that their sheer inability to fight effectively was on full display during the early phase of the invasion. The Allied invasion force had indeed suffered setbacks and blunders during the first landings, but the Italian defense was so poorly executed that the Allies were still able to make significant progress inland and northeastward toward the city of Messina.

The landfall and rapid advance of the Allies caused further problems for the Eastern Front. Reinforcements were needed for the opening of the Italian Front, which meant that vital manpower and resources had to be pulled in order to prevent a complete Italian collapse. Despite the arrival of more German troops and equipment, by late July, the Axis defenders had been pushed all the way back to Messina in the northeastern extreme of the island. Messina was the last major target before the Allies would be able to cross the strait into Calabria, in the southern mainland. By this point, there was little hope of an effective counterattack from their positions in the city, and evacuation was the only realistic option. After Italian leadership discovered that their German allies were planning a full evacuation of their forces, they knew that any hope of defending the city was also lost. They too soon ordered a full evacuation across the sea to the mainland. The Axis evacuation lasted from the 11th to the 17th of August 1943. It was largely successful in saving troops from annihilation, but it had sealed the fate of Italy as well as Benito Mussolini and the Italian fascists.

After Axis presence was surgically removed from the Sicilian island, the Allies were left in possession of a new stronghold and forward operating base even closer to the mainland—and the southern route to Hitler in Berlin. Sicily could be used for several future invasions, so it was a strategically valuable position to fortify. There wasn't too much time to fortify though, as the Allied forces were keen to continue their conquest up to the peninsula. But by this time, many Italians at home already considered the war lost. The Allies had already taken a portion of the country with little effort, and there didn't seem to be much standing in the way of the British and American soldiers' path to Rome. The attitude on the Italian home front was extremely pessimistic and angry. Much of this anger was directed squarely at Benito "Il Duce" Mussolini, the man who had dragged the unprepared Italian nation into a global war under the assumption that their German allies would secure for them an easy victory. Before Sicily even fell, resentment toward the Italian fascist leader had already boiled over. On July 25 of 1943, just over two weeks after Allied landfall in southern Sicily, he was arrested by his own government after being told by both his advisors and the King of Italy, Vittorio Emanuel, that Italy had lost the Second World War. The Italian Grand Council voted him out of office and took him into custody. Eventually, the Italian people themselves would exact their own revenge.

Although he was deeply unpopular by the time he was arrested, Mussolini being ousted from leadership left parts of Italy in severe turmoil, especially those areas soon anticipating Allied arrival. It also caused further issues for the German Reich. Mussolini losing control over Italy meant that Hitler and his Generals needed to send even more German troops to the Italian peninsula in order to prevent a potential switch of allegiances by whatever new government body took power. Italy's military was in ruins, but they could certainly pose a problem for Germany's southern border as well as their holdings in France in the event that their military switched sides as Vichy France's had done after the conquest of North Africa. Hitler was right to worry about this. Dino Grandi, a former ally of Mussolini, had apparently been trying to root out fascism altogether from Italy and its government and wanted to stage a mass attack against the German Nazi troops who were stationed in various areas throughout the peninsula. There had been pro-Allied sentiment cultivating in Italy for some time, and the desire to strike against Germany was not held by Grandi alone.

Italian General Pietro Badoglio was next in line to succeed Mussolini. He initially kept Italy in the war effort, but it was unsustainable. Mussolini was overthrown in part because he had not accepted the reality that the Italian military's capacity to make war on a grand scale had been destroyed since before Operation Torch. If Badoglio wanted to avoid the same fate as Il Duce, he needed to end the fighting. His government eventually signed an armistice with the Allied forces on September 3 of 1943 which, unsurprisingly, deeply angered Hitler. The armistice prompted Hitler to order a mass assault against Italian troops by the

Wehrmacht stationed in the country. It was codenamed Operation Achse and was designed to crush whatever remained of Italy's military capability, so as to prevent a possible Italian incursion across Germany's southern border. Some Italian forces resisted the German attacks, which occurred throughout Italy's holdings, including in the Balkans. They had not received orders to do so, but at this point the military structure was so handicapped that many units were acting independently. The attacks brought much bloodshed, and the fact that the two former Axis allies were now at each other's throats is a testament to the dire position both the German and Italian nations were in.

Operation Achse required even more of Germany's focus to be shifted to Italy to prevent a southern crisis, but it was no use. Italy was soon lost as an Axis ally permanently, and the German Reich was more vulnerable than ever before. Still being pressed from the east, the Nazi war machine would soon be retreating from the south as well. To the west, the Atlantic coastal defenses the Reich had built along the coast of France, the Low Countries, and up toward Scandinavia and northern Germany, still stood strong. But it would not be long before the Western Front, which had been closed and secured since the disastrous fall of France in 1941, was soon to reopen in a major way. By the end of 1944, the many roads leading to Berlin would be clogged with divisions full of eager troops and officers desperate to put an end to the war and to bring the man behind it all to justice.

# D-Day

An Allied invasion of Europe was a long time coming. When it finally came, against southern Italy in 1943, it was met with resounding success and the unambiguous defeat of the German Reich's number one ally. This would not be the final defeat of the Axis, though. For victory to be assured, another new front needed to be opened. It had been discussed for a long time, but France was the most logical target. Just across the English Channel from the British Isles, the coasts of northwestern France made the ideal location for a future base from which to launch operations deeper into Axis territory and exert pressure from the west. It was an important operation. If the Allies failed to secure a foothold in western Europe and their invading forces were annihilated, the war would have dragged on, likely for years to come. The Soviets were making excellent progress but both sides were growing weary, even the recently rejuvenated Red Army soldiers.

The Italian Front could only be pushed so far—northern Italy was a rough and mountainous region dominated by the Swiss Alps, which would have made for a difficult crossing for Allied troops attempting to break out of Italy into central Europe. From the west though, the Allies would be able to secure valuable roads and highways that would provide a quick route to the heart of the Reich, as well as exerting enough pressure to force a weak German response on all three main fronts. This was needed in order to force a timely collapse of Hitler's regime. If success was to be had on the French coast, though, the Allies needed to be able to learn lessons from history, something Hitler and his Generals had long struggled to do.

## Lessons From Dieppe

Before a seaborne invasion of France could even be considered, the Allies' capability to conduct naval raids and landings needed extensive testing. The idea of launching an invasion to retake mainland Europe had been discussed ever since the Battle of Britain ended in Allied success, but an effective invasion would remain infeasible until years later. Still, preparations were being made and intelligence was being gathered. Well before the invasion of Italy and North Africa began, the Allies were doing stress tests to see how fiercely the Germans would defend the French coast, and how much Allied forces could withstand while trying to push inland. In August of 1942, one of the most dramatic mock-invasions took place in the northern French port city of Dieppe. That summer, the Allies launched a seaborne raid into the French port, which was meant to be captured and held for a short time before being abandoned.

There were many reasons for the raid on Dieppe, one of which was to placate Joseph Stalin and the Soviets. By the summer of 1942, the Soviets had won the Battle of Moscow, but the Red Army was still in rough condition, and the Battle of Stalingrad was soon to begin. Their forces were exhausted, and at this point, it must have seemed like the world was on their shoulders. Aside from the skirmishes in the North African desert and the other African colonies south of the Sahara, the Red Army was the only thing keeping the German war machine in check. They desperately needed relief from the brunt of the Wehrmacht's force and had for some time been begging the Allied forces to open a second front in Germany's west or south in order to relieve the exhausted

Soviet defense effort. The Allies remained hesitant for years to commit to anything significant, and Dieppe was certainly not what the Soviets had been hoping for. Indeed, it was never meant to actually open a new front, but it did signal to Stalin that they were working on something. At most, it would only ever be harassment or annoyance. The main purpose of Dieppe was rather to gather intelligence, gauge the German response, and to test the feasibility of a larger-scale invasion. Essentially, Dieppe was an experiment or testing ground, and Canadian soldiers were selected as the apparent guinea pigs.

On August 19 of 1942, an Allied force consisting of overwhelmingly Canadian troops landed around the port town as part of the raid codenamed Operation Jubilee. They were meant to quickly seize and secure the surrounding area and destroy the port facilities before making their planned retreat back across the English Channel. Given the presence of Axis forces in the region, holding Dieppe for an extended period of time was untenable. But even the limited goals of the 2nd Canadian Infantry Division and their commander, Major-General John Roberts, were unachievable. Earlier, Hitler had instructed his Generals that any port landings by Allied forces against Europe were to be treated as the initiation of a full-scale invasion and were to be met with the fullest defensive response that could be mustered. The Luftwaffe in particular were instructed to make a full-hearted defense of the coast. The Allies had anticipated a spirited response but were still unprepared for the full weight of the Luftwaffe over German-controlled skies.

The Allied forces landed across several beaches codenamed by various colors. At every landing point, they faced setbacks and repeatedly failed to meet their objectives. At both White and Red beaches, armored tank support for the infantry were late arriving, leaving the infantry regiments stranded on the beach, pinned down by suppressing fire. Few of the landing forces here were able to push into the town itself. The Canadian forces at Blue beach fared little better. They could destroy neither the German machine gun placements on the beachhead nor their artillery, leaving the troops vulnerable and stuck in place for the entirety of the operation. The only successful venture in the Dieppe raid took place at Orange beach, one of the two beaches stormed by British commandos. They were the only ones able to achieve their goals and evacuate the coastal area on time—everywhere else was a disaster. The RAF was unable to help the situation and they took heavy losses as well, losing over 100 of their aircraft. The Luftwaffe suffered less than half those losses.

Overall, Dieppe was a debacle that, at the time, seemed to have virtually no redeeming value. Numbers of casualties vary, but the Allies suffered severe losses, with thousands being killed in action or taken as POWs and of those who were fortunate enough to make it back to England, thousands more were severely wounded. The Canadian soldiers suffered the vast majority of these losses. Again, German casualties did not even approach these kinds of numbers and they were able to repel a larger invading force with relative ease. Despite this troubling state of affairs, there was value in the failure and there were plenty of lessons to be learned, many of which would be used in the successful landings in North Africa and Sicily, and later, in France once again. Operation Jubilee was an inauspicious start to the Canadian military's involvement in the

European theater of war (they had previously been active in Asia), but their sacrifice was not in vain.

First, the Allies witnessed firsthand how disastrous an amphibious landing could be when confined to a small port with a narrow front. Although the raid took place across six portions of beach, the area of operations was too dense for an effective foray into a fortified zone, and the German defenders were easily able to destroy or completely suppress and cripple incoming invaders. Further, the Allies realized that it was absolutely vital that whenever they would be able to launch a mass invasion into Europe, it needed to be a surprise. This was a tall task, given the fact that Hitler was hyper-aware that he still had a formidable and apparently uninvadable enemy lying just off of his coast, but it would need to be done. Prior Axis knowledge of the Dieppe raid had doomed any hopes of securing the landing points and it certainly would do so again in the event of an even larger operation.

The several setbacks that plagued the Canadian armored tank units also turned out to be a blessing in disguise. The tanks used at Dieppe had endless trouble navigating the beach areas and making their way into town, struggling to gain traction on the rocky and pebble-filled terrain. When D-Day finally arrived, the tanks the Allies employed were heavily adapted since the Dieppe debacle, and they were able to much more effectively storm beaches alongside Allied infantry units. Finally, the Allies learned that amphibious assaults directly on or near ports were too risky, despite ports being a valuable strategic asset worth capturing early on. Ports were generally defended much more heavily than stretches of coastline, and the structures surrounding them made them easier to defend.

Although coastal beach targets made for rougher initial landings due to the general lack of nearby infrastructure, Allied leadership realized they were more conducive to long-term success. The Allied leadership of the Americans and British Commonwealth after Dieppe had done what Hitler and his Generals had failed to do after the siege of Moscow. They had learned from their mistakes and were committed to correcting them when it came time to land in France once again.

### The Quebec Conference and Operation Overlord

On August 17 of 1943, just days after the Axis powers had initiated their evacuation of the island of Sicily, the Allied powers met in Quebec, Canada at a gathering hosted by Canadian Prime Minister W. L. M. King. It was a crucial moment across every theater in the war, and several issues needed to be discussed. Both President Roosevelt and Prime Minister Churchill were in attendance, but Joseph Stalin had refused to leave his people during a critical moment in the defense of the Soviet Union. The conference lasted until the 24th of August and several matters were decided. Two of these had especially significant ramifications for the future of the war. For one, British and American leaders had agreed to further develop their joint efforts in developing a new weapon of unprecedented destructive power. The so-called Manhattan Project had technically begun in 1939 but became a serious focus in 1942. It included the contributions of American, British, and Canadian scientists and the weapon they had been developing was the world's first atomic bomb, to be considered for use in exceptional circumstances. At the Quebec Conference,

Roosevelt and Churchill worked out the details and ground rules regarding the future use of their creation.

In Quebec, the Allies also discussed immediate next moves in the European campaign. By the conclusion of the conference in late August, the leaders had agreed, and the decision was made to launch an invasion of western Europe and take the fight directly to Germany. Finally, American high command, many of whom had been pressing incessantly to attack Germany as soon as possible, had gotten their wish. The invasion was set to launch from the British Isles, but the landing site still needed to be determined. Selecting the ideal location was crucial, one of the cruel lessons learned at Dieppe. If the Germans correctly reasoned where the invasion was to occur, it would be doomed before the Allies ever left British shores.

The French city of Calais, an important port, was the most obvious choice. It was the closest point between France and Great Britain and so would require less time at sea, and it was also close to significant road and rail access which would provide a quick route to the French interior and beyond to Berlin. But an invasion at Calais was exactly what the German defenders would be expecting. This wouldn't do—Operation Overlord, as the Allied invasion and liberation came to be known, needed to take the Germans by surprise. Plus, Calais was very well-defended and was a focal point of Germany's coastal fortress defenses, so an attempt to push inland into the city from here would be fraught with risks.

Brittany, a French peninsular region in the country's northwest, was also considered but ultimately the region of Normandy was selected, which lay between Calais and Brittany.

Choosing a location other than the most obvious one wasn't enough, though. The Allies, in fact, went to great lengths to convince the Germans that Calais was indeed their true target. The success of this strategy meant that when their forces landed at their real destinations along Normandy, they would not be facing the full weight of the Nazi defense and would be able to make gains inland before the Wehrmacht could respond to stop it. Originally, Operation Neptune, which was the codename for the specific amphibious landing portion of the broader Operation Overlord, was scheduled to begin earlier in 1944 but after several delays, it was eventually decided to launch in early June of that year. Even if the Germans were fooled as to the location of Allied landing and chose not to strike at a heavily defended port, more preliminary steps would be necessary to ensure success. Since the victory at the Battle of Britain and the end of the Blitz, the British had been carrying out air raids and bombings on German positions. In the lead up to D-Day, though, these campaigns were intensified in order to soften German resistance once the invasion got underway. French Resistance members operating within occupied territory and carrying out both espionage and sabotage operations were also a boon to the Allies who would be contending with an enemy fighting itself.

*The German city of Cologne after the war, completely demolished by*
*Allied bombing*

The bombing prior to D-Day also served another purpose—
to draw the Luftwaffe away from the Eastern Front. After it was
realized the Dieppe was categorically not the opening of a second
front that the Soviets had been hoping for, the intense bombings
served to create a kind of "synthetic" second front which would
be able to pull air support, but likely not infantry, away from the far
eastern battles. The RAF began targeting only military and industrial
zones but eventually began striking populated civilian targets as
well with incendiary explosives. The decision was controversial
and, by any standards, a war crime, but it was neither the first nor
the last to be committed over the course of the Second World
War. The decision to strike civilian areas was, of course, made
in order to damage German morale, but it's debatable whether

these attacks weakened or sharpened morale on the home front. It certainly was successful in convincing many Germans that the war needed to end as soon as possible, but an actual amphibious landing and invasion would still be a prerequisite to victory in Europe—ultimate success against Hitler simply would not come by way of aerial bombardment.

Aside from strategic considerations, things were looking good for the Allies in terms of sheer force of power. A major prerequisite to a successful amphibious invasion of occupied France was the guarantee of Allied air superiority, which had been assured by 1943 when much of the Luftwaffe was tied up in the east and those units in the west were being continuously lured out by the RAF to their destruction. When the time came, British and American air squadrons would have a much easier time supporting both their navy and landing crews. The Allies also already had decisive naval superiority over the Germans, who would have a difficult time preventing any cross-channel operations, even with their infamous and feared U-boat submarines. As long as the formidable Royal Navy was present, Allied troops were going to land on those French beaches and there was little the German seaborne forces could do about it. The only uncertain matter was the task of progressing off of those beaches. The massive length of the coastline that Germany had to defend also boded well for the Allies. This territory stretched the entirety of the French, Lowland, German, and Norwegian coastline which both gave the Allies plenty of options for potential invasion sites and forced the German defenders to spread their forces thinly over a huge area.

The planning for the operation wasn't problem-free for the Allies though. Dwight D. Eisenhower, the American General and Supreme Commander of Allied forces in Europe, had to deal with two opposing subordinates, American General George Patton and British Field Marshal Bernard Montgomery, who had conflicting opinions as to how Operation Overlord was to be conducted. Eventually though, differences were put aside and the details for the invasion were ironed out before the time came to take to the sea. By the time planning concluded, the invasion was set to begin June 6 of 1944, with a target area consisting of a stretch of coast roughly 50 miles long. Again, the Allies were taking pointers from Dieppe—they needed to avoid a too-narrow beach landing and to spread as far apart as was feasible (i.e., while still allowing for the invading forces to successfully and reasonably support each other) in order to prevent a mass concentration of German defenders. Five beaches were selected, not too far apart from each other, for the combined American, British, and Canadian forces who had begun to amass across the English Channel in the British Isles. By the night of the invasion, over 150,000 Allied troops had mustered and were idling in Britain, waiting eagerly for the order to launch the greatest, most important battle in human history.

### June 6, 1944

In the first week of June 1944, 156,000 Allied troops set sail from Britain with the goal of liberating the French from German occupation and beginning the long march toward the German heartland. This initial invasion force was heavily supported by both air and sea. The Allied navies and air forces both supported troops as they landed and pushed inland, bombarding German positions to soften the resistance prior to disembarking. Out of the five beaches in total that the Allies stormed that day, the Germans were able to prevent their advance at exactly zero of them—while it did not go off without a hitch, it was a success that echoed through the remainder of the war. The American forces were tasked with two beaches on D-Day ("D-Day" has since become synonymous with Operation Overlord and Operation Neptune, but in military terms, D-Day simply refers to the day a battle or invasion began. June 6 was D-Day, June 7 was D+1, etc.), the westernmost beaches codenamed Utah and Omaha. The eastern beaches, codenamed Sword and Gold, were given to the British armies. Sandwiched between the two British landing sites was Juno beach, which was set to be invaded by the Canadians. The decision to land on the beaches away from heavily defended ports (as was the case during the Dieppe raid) was wise, but the Allies needed to capture a port not too long after landing in order for the invaders to be effectively resupplied and reinforced.

The numerous fronts that Germany was now facing required that the Wehrmacht be spread thin and flung far across the European continent, which the Allies were counting on. By the time D-Day took place, the German Reich had committed twenty divisions to the southern portion of Europe (Italy) as well as a whopping 200 divisions devoted to the Eastern Front against the Soviet Union, leaving only sixty divisions available to defend against the new western assault. From here they had to cover the entire coastline, despite the fact that German intelligence fully anticipated an assault against occupied France. The other hindering factor was the aforementioned extreme lengths the Allies went to to convince the Axis the invasion was occurring elsewhere. They employed extensive fake radio chatter with fabricated orders and communications to reaffirm the German belief that Calais was the actual destination. The British even created massive inflatable decoy tanks which they gathered and moved around at ports adjacent to Calais and left them out in the open for potential Axis reconnaissance to witness. This convinced the Germans not only that Calais was chosen, but that the invasion was likely imminent. Fake paratroopers were also used, being dropped deep behind enemy lines in various areas to draw German attention away from the coastal Allied landing sites.

*A photo from within an American landing craft*

Despite possessing a relatively smaller portion of Germany's full fighting force, the defenders on the beaches on D-Day fought hard and were able to inflict heavy losses on the Allies at all five beach landings. The American beaches saw heavy casualties, particularly Omaha beach to the east of Utah. Omaha's beach was long, meaning that American forces would have to trek up the long and sandy beach under continuous machine gun and artillery fire. Further ahead on the beach were massive, steep plateaus which provided natural defenses for the Germans. The Nazis had constructed their defenses and machine gun nests atop these plateaus and were able to fire downward on advancing troops even before they disembarked from their landing crafts. Casualties at Omaha were immediately so heavy that the German defenders pre-emptively declared the beachhead to be secure. The Americans continued their push, though, and although they advanced very little on the first day, they were able to capture the beachhead by midnight. Utah beach was far easier going for the Americans by comparison, as Utah did not have the extensive buildup of defenses that Omaha had (Omaha was by far the most heavily defended of the beaches), and troops were able to clear pathways for more troops and armor with relative ease. The British and Canadians also fared a bit better, especially at the British Gold beach and the Canadian Juno. The forces here were the only two that were able to accomplish all their goals and successfully link up on the first day of the operation. Juno beach was another difficult landing site that was also heavily defended, but their naval support was able to pierce a large hole in the German defenses from the sea, through which the Canadians could surge and overwhelm the German defenders.

*Normandy during the June invasions*

After the highly successful landings on Juno and Gold, the Allies were able to liberate the French town of Bayeux the following day. These two beaches were linked quickly, and most of the rest of the week was spent making connections between all five beachheads to create a single united front along the coast, which was accomplished by the 12th of June, six days after first landing (D+6). The Allies also began pushing toward the Cotentin peninsula (a smaller peninsula to the east of the larger Brittany peninsula) and the upcoming Battle of Caen. On June 18, the battle began in earnest with the participation of American, British, and Canadian troops. It was an intense fight, and the Germans committed a large portion of their available panzer units to the defense of the city, meaning it was destructive for both the Allies and Germany. Finally, in early August, the city was completely occupied by Allied troops. Meanwhile, American forces had secured the Cotentin peninsula and captured the city of Cherbourg. Cherbourg afforded the Allies a vital and reliable port from which they could draw resupplies, while the successful capture of Caen allowed for the D-Day offensive forces to finally stage a breakthrough out of their initial landing sites and into the interior.

The operation proceeded quickly from there, and within three months of D-Day the Allies had pushed German forces all the way back to the Seine, a river in northern France that runs through Paris. By late August of 1944, the struggle for the liberation of Paris, a city which had been in German hands since June of 1940, was underway. At around the same time the Allies were approaching the Paris city limits, the French Resistance forces within decided to make their move. They began attacking German forces and conducting sabotage missions just as the Nazis were preparing to defend the city. Initially the Americans had planned on simply encircling and laying siege to the city but did not intend on invading and occupying it until later in the campaign, believing that an attempt to take Paris at this stage would only slow Allied progress. Charles de Gaulle disagreed and tried to convince Eisenhower that the city would be taken easily and wouldn't hinder the rest of the campaign. Eisenhower wasn't convinced, but de Gaulle was implacable. In 1943, the French military formed the French 2nd Armored Division, which had joined the liberation effort in France sometime after the initial invasion. The division was led by General Jacques-Philippe Leclerc, but de Gaulle had enough power over French forces to be able to command Leclerc in his operations. This is exactly what de Gaulle threatened to do if the Allies chose to cut a path around Paris instead—he would detach the 2nd Armored Division and Leclerc and send them into Paris on their own. For these reasons, Eisenhower eventually acquiesced, and the Allies geared up for an invasion into the city.

Charles de Gaulle turned out to be right about the speed at which the defenses in Paris would crumble. When the Allies began pressing into the city on the 23rd of August, it would take only two days before German forces either fled from their positions, were killed, or surrendered to the French and American liberators. They officially ceded the city to the provisional French government that was being set up under de Gaulle, and Dietrich von Choltitz, the German General in charge of Paris, was taken into Allied custody. It was another great upset to Hitler, who had ordered von Choltitz to fight to the death in the defense of Paris, despite the relative lack of troops, armor, and defensive structures. Just like General Friedrich Paulus during the Battle of Stalingrad, von Choltitz chose to surrender rather than condemn his men to a pointless death. It wasn't the only order he disobeyed either. Hitler also had condemned the entire city, famous landmarks and all, to destruction in the event that the Germans could not protect it from the Allies. Choltitz had prepared their destruction in advance, placing explosive caches underneath vital infrastructure as well as wonders like the Eiffel Tower, but in the end, he refused to do it. It's unknown exactly why von Choltitz chose to defy Hitler in that moment, but perhaps he felt that history was already going to be treating him and his people poorly, and he did not need to add the destruction of the most admired city on earth to the list of grievances against the German Reich. Or perhaps he was just too sentimental. In any case, Paris was in Allied hands, fully intact.

After the Allies secured Paris, they continued to move quickly to push the Axis out of France and press toward Germany. By the six-month mark of Operation Overlord, the Germans were all but completely removed from France. Another naval invasion, Operation Dragoon on France's southern coast, was launched in mid-August and was marked a success by the end of August. For the first time in four years, France was once again a democratic nation. After the war, Philippe Pétain was tried by the new French government for treason against its people. He was found guilty and originally condemned to death, but he ended up remaining in custody for the rest of his life. Charles de Gaulle, on the other hand, would go down in history as one of the men who was key in liberating the proud French nation from the grips of the tyrannical Nazi dictator in Berlin. That was his legacy, but it did not yet have time to be crafted. For now, the Allies put down the Battle of Paris as a "win" and continued the push to Berlin.

On the Eastern Front, the Germans had already spectacularly failed their last great offensive with the Battle of Kursk in 1943. But their last great offensive in the west was still to be held, and it too would be a disaster. The so-called Battle of the Bulge (also known as the Battle of the Ardennes or the Ardennes Offensive) was one of the largest battles of the entire Western Front and like Kursk, it represented the last time the German Reich would be able to conduct a large offensive operation in that respective theater. The battle began in mid-December of 1944 and continued into January of 1945, it took place in the Ardennes region between Belgium and

Luxembourg. It was a desperate, last-ditch effort to turn the tides of the Western Front, reverse the Allied advance, split the Allied offensive force into pieces, and finally recapture the vital city of Antwerp in Belgium. The German attackers vastly outnumbered the Americans in the Ardennes, having put everything they had into this offensive, which the Germans codenamed Operation Autumn Mist. They incurred heavy losses to the American defenders, but once again resupply and reinforcement capacity won the day. The Americans were able to increase their presence of tanks, equipment and manpower at a rate that vastly outpaced what the Wehrmacht were capable of. By this point, the equipment the Axis was fielding was of poorer quality than what the Allies were producing, anyway.

In the end, the German attack at the Ardennes was another embarrassing failure and resulted in yet another blow to German morale. Once weather conditions allowed for it, American aircraft were able to strike at the exposed German units with ease, reversing the fortunes of the American troops on the ground and cementing their victory. German hopes of turning the tables and retaking the land they had won in 1940 were now dead, a feeling that German military command had become all too familiar with after the several crushing defeats in Russia, Ukraine, and North Africa. More Germans than ever considered the war a lost cause, and the German population was growing discontented. If that weren't bad enough, the huge force mustered for the Battle of the Bulge required even more troops to be pulled from other vital areas including the east. This was pleasing to Stalin, but for the Germans it meant they had handicapped one of their own front lines and earned exactly nothing for their troubles. This single loss meant that both German fronts were now more doomed than ever.

German ground forces were reeling badly after the loss at the Ardennes, but their air force was faring little better. The use of the supremely powerful American-made P-51 Mustang fighter bomber had allowed for the Allied air forces to "deliver a death blow to the Luftwaffe" at the Battle of the Bulge (Newland & Chun, 2011). The once mighty and feared Luftwaffe had apparently gone the way of the German panzer divisions, who had fallen from grace during the Soviet campaign. The German military had shocked the world in 1939 and 1940 with their new ways of making war and their blitzkrieg tactics, but by 1944 it was painfully obvious that their war machine had severely stagnated, and the Allies wartime development and production had irrevocably eclipsed that of the Nazis. It was only a matter of time before the German command structure collapsed in on itself entirely, and more than one Axis General held the opinion that Germany needed to surrender if it wanted to survive. Still, as the Allies continued to advance, Hitler was vehemently opposed to surrender. As a result, the war in Europe dragged on for far longer than it needed to.

Once the German attackers were shattered, the road to Berlin was cleared for the Allied armies. As the Americans, British, and Soviets were approaching the city, Hitler was in a panicked rage. He blamed the German people for failing to live up to his vision for them and believed he had surrounded himself with incompetent Generals. In reality, it was Hitler's refusal to listen to his Generals and his poor decision-making when it came to selecting battles and opening new fronts that had doomed the Reich's global fascist ambitions. But nothing could sway Hitler from his new, fierce contempt for the German people that he believed had betrayed both him and the fatherland. In April of 1945, as the Allies were mere weeks away from entering the Nazi capital, Hitler decided that he was not going to be taken alive and he would not surrender. He would do what his Generals Paulus and von Choltitz were too cowardly to do. He would take his own life and order the suicides of several of his top Generals and advisors. He would accomplish this with his new mistress-turned-bride Eva Braun in his Berlin bunker by biting into a toxic cyanide capsule while simultaneously shooting himself. Hitler was dead, but not before he ordered the destruction and firebombing of Berlin as punishment to the German people for their weak will. This order was never carried out, but it shows the degree of despondency and rage he was feeling in his final days. The führer was dead, perhaps the most significant outcome of D-Day, which was a catalyst for the implosion of the Reich. Only after Hitler was gone were more level-headed commanders able to take control of the government and finally negotiate an end to the Second World War.

In early May, the Soviet Red Army, led by Field Marshal Zhukov, flooded into the German capital city of Berlin. On their long road there, the Soviets committed horrific war crimes against both the Polish and German populations as retribution for the war crimes the Nazis had committed against the Soviets. As much as the soldiers suffered between 1939 and 1945, the war was most brutal on the European civilian population, particularly those unfortunate enough to have lived in the lands between Hitler and Stalin. These areas were by far the most brutally affected by the war and suffered atrocities from both advancing armies. Though the Red Army's journey to Berlin could best be described as a villainous trek, they were now prepared to put an end to the German Reich permanently, and along the way, it was Soviet troops that liberated many of the German death camps holding Jewish prisoners. The most infamous of the sites, the Auschwitz-Birkenau camp, was liberated by Red Army soldiers in late January of 1945. The Holocaust, one of the greatest atrocities in human history, was finally coming to an end after claiming the lives of millions of Europe's Jews. By the second day of May, the Soviets had cut down the Nazi flag from atop the German Reichstag and raised up their own banner of the hammer and sickle in its place. Just days later, German General Alfred Jodl offered terms of unconditional surrender to the Allied forces advancing from the west. The next day, Field Marshal Wilhelm Keitel offered the same terms to the Soviets who had pierced Berlin from the east.

*A modern photo of the Auschwitz-Birkenau Nazi death camp, decades after its liberation by the Soviet 322nd Rifle Division*

# CONCLUSION

At long last, the war in Europe was over. Though the global future outlook was grim after the unbelievable victories of the Wehrmacht in 1939, 1940, and 1941, the combined willpower of the British in North Africa, the Soviets at Stalingrad and Kursk, and the Americans in France was enough to grind the greatest war machine the world had yet produced to a screeching halt. The Japanese stubbornly refused to surrender as their German and Italian allies had done, and so the war raged on in the Pacific, but Victory in Europe (also known as V-E Day) was monumental in the global war against fascism. Although the Allied forces that landed in Normandy in June of 1944 were not the ones that eventually captured Berlin, the pressure they exerted on Germany's western region allowed the Soviets breathing room to march on the capital more easily. D-Day and the Soviet advance were mutually beneficial—Operation Overlord aided the progress of the Soviet advance, but it was the Soviet advance demanding so much of the Wehrmacht and Luftwaffe's combined attention that allowed for the success of Overlord in the first place. D-Day was a monumental achievement that brought a rapid end to the most destructive war in history, and "there will never be another operation like Overlord again" (Morgan, 1996).

The Allies were now focused on restoring European democracy and deciding what to do with the failed German state. The Soviets wanted to utterly demilitarize and deindustrialize the country so that its people could no longer wage war against Europe (the memory of the First World War still lingered). The United States had a different view, believing a democratic Germany would be a strong future ally, particularly against the Soviet Union, with whom the United States foresaw a coming conflict. In the end, Germany was divided up between the world powers and eventually consolidated into the capitalist West Germany and the communist East Germany, a puppet of the Soviet Union. Berlin itself was also partitioned between the Allies and the Soviets. But before the Allies could focus on these post-war details, the matter of the Japanese Empire still needed to be solved. The eventual fall of Japan had been a foregone conclusion for some time—their military capacity had severely deteriorated since the Battle of Midway, and they would be unable to turn the tide with the production and resource discrepancy between the Japanese and American militaries. The only question remaining was how and when Japan would fall, and whether or not they could ever force a surrender. The Germans had surrendered before it became necessary to use the Allies' ultimate weapon developed in the Manhattan Project, but for several reasons, Japan provided a suitable opportunity. Before this was considered, however, several more key battles were to take place in the Pacific theater.

The Battle of Saipan from June 15 through to early July was staged almost concurrently with Operation Overlord. It is even often referred to as "Pacific D-Day," although Saipan did not involve an invasion of the Japanese home islands. Saipan was originally not intended as a valuable war target but was eventually deemed vital as it would give the Americans a critical naval base close to Japanese home waters and allow for the stationing of B-29 Superfortress bombers (introduced in 1944 as a replacement for the famous B-17 Flying Fortress), which placed them within realistic bombing range of Japan. The eventual successful capture of Saipan gave the Allies control over the Mariana Islands to the south of the Japanese archipelago. The defeat caused serious distress on the home front and prompted Japanese leader Hideki Tojo to resign from office.

The year 1945 brought more significant losses for Emperor Hirohito's military. After Saipan was captured and American bombers housed there, the next logical major target was Iwo Jima, an island roughly between Saipan in the Marianas and Japan. Iwo Jima was home to many Japanese fighters which would harass and destroy American bombers during flights to Japan from Saipan, and so, it needed to be neutralized. Once Iwo Jima was captured, the Americans would be able to use it to instead house their own fighters, which could then escort said bombers on their missions. The battle lasted from February 19 of 1945 to the end of March that year, and it also happened to be a foregone conclusion. The Japanese were at a severe disadvantage in terms of both technology of equipment and air superiority, and they had no hope of retreat from the island once things began to go south. Despite this, the

Japanese on Iwo Jima fought hard and inflicted heavy losses on the American invaders, with many choosing to fight to the death rather than be taken prisoner. Although the Americans won the day, the brutality of the battle made many Americans question at what cost eventual victory in the Pacific would come.

*A monument of American soldiers planting their flag on Iwo Jima*

Taking Iwo Jima allowed for the subsequent invasion of Okinawa, an island even closer to mainland Japan. The Battle of Okinawa lasted from April 1 to June 22 of 1945 and is most noteworthy for how severe American casualties were. Okinawa was very close to the Japanese home islands and as a result, the defensive effort was incredibly fierce, and the defenders were focused on making American losses as significant as possible. Indeed, by the time Allied victory was secured, American losses were nearly unbearable and necessitated an alternative to the planned invasion of the home islands. If the Japanese defended

Okinawa so vigorously, bloodshed in the homeland would be infinitely worse. American leadership was correct to worry—the Japanese government was anticipating an invasion of the islands, and instead of surrendering, they had been preparing civilians to fight with improvised weapons and were planning on mass suicide bombing campaigns to drive out the would-be invaders. It was Okinawa that, above all, led the Allies to the conclusion that something else would need to be done to force Japanese surrender.

So it was that on the morning of the 6th of August 1945, the American B29 bomber named "Enola Gay" took off on its mission to drop an atomic bomb on the Japanese city of Hiroshima. It was the first nuclear device ever used in the field of battle, and the second was soon to follow. The Hiroshima bomb was the smaller of the two, nicknamed "Little Boy." Just days later on August 9, the larger "Fat Man" atomic bomb was dropped on the city of Nagasaki after the first bomb had still failed to force a surrender. Both cities were utterly devastated. Both bombers had taken off from the Marianas, from airfields the Americans had won just months earlier. After the second Japanese city was leveled, the Americans were finally able to occupy the country without a single battle taking place on the home islands. On September 2, the Japanese government issued their official surrender to Allied forces.

Outside of Spain, European and global fascism on a large scale was now dead. It was a victory for democracy, but it came at a devastating cost. Much of Europe was in ruins by 1945 and the human toll of the conflict across the globe was staggering. Several European economies would remain in crisis for years even with massive financial aid from the United States, who emerged from the war in a far stronger position than any of their European allies, having remained out of the conflict for years and being physically distant from the main theater of war. The task of rebuilding the world (and several of the world's governments) was now at hand, but the world would be forever different. War would never be the same again. When the world saw the destructive power of the atomic bomb, this was clear enough to see. The First World War back in 1914 had changed warfare with its brutal and prolonged trench combat which shattered young soldiers' visions of quick wars with glorious victories, and the Second World War changed everything yet again with its massive, global implications and unprecedented cruelty against civilian populations. The genocide against Europe's Jewish people had come to an end, but the memory remains to this day. After the introduction of atomic weapons, the world feared for what was to come next. It was perhaps possible, many thought, that the next global conflict of similar scale could very well be the end of civilization. The atomic bomb, one of the most consequential products of the Second World War and its battles, embodied the fears of an American generation for over a decade.

The reasons for using the atomic bombs in the first place were numerous. On the one hand, the Americans desperately wanted to avoid the inevitable carnage and mass casualties that would almost certainly accompany a naval invasion of the main islands. More important though, was that when the dust finally settled from the war, the Soviet Union would be in a position to steamroll the entirety of Europe and much of Asia. By 1945 they were already deep into central Europe and just a day before the Fat Man bomb was dropped, they had declared war on the empire and stormed across the border, down Japanese-controlled Korea and toward Japan. They would have likely made a spirited offensive against the home islands, given their rapid progress, if not for prompt Japanese surrender (in fact, many believe that it was in fact the Soviet invasion that forced the Japanese surrender, not the use of American atomic bombs).

In order to prevent the Soviet Union, whom the United States and Britain viewed as an inevitable future enemy, from dominating Europe and gaining more Asian territory, the atomic bombs were deployed in order to showcase the destructive power of the American air force to the Soviets. With a weapon capable of annihilating cities, the United States wanted to deter the Soviets from capitalizing on their advantageous position over a Europe in crisis. Although the Soviets did halt their military operations on a large scale after both Germany and Japan surrendered unconditionally, the world was now dominated by just two superpowers: the USA and the USSR, the latter of which would, in short time, be in possession of their own arsenal of nuclear weapons. The end of World War II was the beginning of a far longer, far more complex conflict—the Cold War and the global nuclear arms race, which would hold the world at the brink of destruction for over four decades.

Dear Valued Readers,

I want to express my heartfelt gratitude to each one of you who has dedicated their time to delve into the pages of "The Greatest Battles of World War II. A World at War: World War II Battles that Shaped the Course of History." Your interest in exploring the pivotal battles of WWII and understanding the far-reaching consequences of each engagement is deeply appreciated. It's your support that fuels the passion for sharing historical knowledge, and I hope the book has enriched your understanding of this transformative period in human history.

If you've found the book to be an insightful journey through the annals of World War II, I kindly request you to consider leaving a review or star rating on Amazon by following the link below, or using the QR code. Your feedback is invaluable, not only to me as an author but also to fellow readers seeking guidance in their literary pursuits. Your reviews contribute to the book's visibility and help others discover its historical significance. Once again, thank you for your time, your engagement, and your dedication to understanding the past.

Warm regards,
Alexander L Sheppard

https://www.amazon.com/dp/B0CJ45V9H8

# REFERENCES

Baird, J. (1969). The myth of Stalingrad. *Journal of Contemporary History* 4(3), 187-204.

Barbier, M. (2007). *D-Day Deception: Operation Fortitude and the Normandy Invasion.* Westport: Praeger Security International.

Baxter, I.M. & Volstad, R. (2004). *Battle of Stalingrad: Russia's Great Patriotic War.* Hong Kong: Concord Publications.

Bell, L. (1970). The Failure of Nazism in America: The German American Bund, 193-1941. *Political Science Quarterly* 85(4), 585-599.

Bongers, A. & Torres, J. (2020). Revisiting the Battle of Midway. *Military Operations Research* 25(2), 49-68.

Bourke, J. (2001). *The Second World War: A People's History.* Oxford: Oxford University Press.

Brustein, W. & King, R. (2004). Anti-Semitism in Europe Before the Holocaust. *International Political Science Review* 25(1), 35-53.

Clairmont, F. (2003). Stalingrad: Hitler's Nemesis. *Economic and Political Weekly* 38(27), 2819-2823.

Coox, A. (1994). The Pearl Harbor Raid Revisited. *Journal of American-East Asian Relations* 3(3), 211-227.

*D-Day's Parachuting Dummies and Inflatable Tanks.* (n.d.) Imperial War Museum. https://www.iwm.org.uk/history/d-days-parachuting-dummies-and-inflatable-tanks#:~:text=Fake%20 radio%20traffic%20and%20decoy,and%20after%20the%20 Normandy%20landings.

Diamond, J. (2017). *Images of War: The Invasion of Sicily in 1943*. South Yorkshire: Pen & Sword Military.

Dick, R. (1990). Battle of Britain. *Air Power History* 37(2), 11-25.

Engle, E. & Paananen, L. (1992). *The Winter War: The Soviet Attack on Finland 1939-1940*. Mechanicsburg: Stackpole Books.

Evans, R. J. (2004). *The Coming of the Third Reich*. New York: Penguin Press.

Fitzpatrick, M. & Moses, A.D. (2018, Aug. 19). *Nazism, Socialism, and the Falsification of History*. ABC. https://www.abc.net.au/religion/ nazism-socialism-and-the-falsification-of-history/10214302

Frank, W. (1987). The Spanish Civil War and the Coming Second World War. *International History Review* 9(3), 368-409.

Hammond, B. (2012). *El-Alamein: The Battle That Turned the Tide of the Second World War*. Osprey Publishing.

Hanson, V. D. (2003). *Ripples of Battle*. New York: Doubleday.

Irvine, W. (1996). Domestic Politics and the Fall of France in 1940. *Historical Reflections* 22(1), 77-90.

Mann, C. & Jorgensen, C. (2002). *Hitler's Arctic War: The German Campaigns in Norway, Finland, and the USSR 1940-1945*. Surrey: Ian Allen Publishing.

Merridale, C. (2006). Culture, Ideology, and Combat in the Red Army, 1939-45. *Journal of Contemporary History* 41(2), 305-324.

Morgan, T. (1996). D-Day at Normandy Revisited. *Army History* (36), 30-35.

Newland, S.J. & Chun, C.K. (2011). *The European campaign: Its Origins and Conduct*. Strategic Studies Institute.

Paine, S.C.M. (2017). *The Japanese Empire: Grand Strategy from the Meiji Restoration to the Pacific War*. Cambridge: Cambridge University Press.

Parshall, J. (2005). *Shattered Sword: The untold story of the Battle of Midway*. Washington, D.C.: Potomac Books.

Pleshakov, C. (2006). *Stalin's Folly: The Tragic First Ten Days of World War II on the Eastern Front*. New York: First Mariner Books.

Royde-Smith, J.G. (n.d.). *Costs of the War: Killed, Wounded, Prisoners, or Missing*. Britannica. https://www.britannica.com/event/World-War-II/Human-and-material-cost

Sadkovich, J. (1989). Understanding Defeat: Reappraising Italy's Role in World War II. *Journal of Contemporary History* 24(1), 27-61.

Schneider, F. & Gullans, C. (1961). Last letters from Stalingrad. *The Hudson Review* 14(3), 335-367.

Stahel, D. (2015). *The battle for Moscow*. Cambridge: Cambridge University Press.

Summerfield, P. (2010). Dunkirk and the Popular Memory of Britain at War, 1940-58. *Journal of Contemporary History* 45(4), 788-811.

Todd, D. (2016, Feb. 25). *Lest We Overlook the 'Asian Holocaust.'* Vancouver Sun. https://vancouversun.com/news/metro/douglas-todd-lest-we-overlook-the-asian-holocaust

Toeppel, R. (2018). *Kursk 1943: The Greatest Battle of the Second World War*. Warwick: Helion and Company Ltd.

Zahniser, M. (1992). Rethinking the Significance of Disaster: The United States and the Fall of France in 1940. *International History Review* 14(2). 252-276.

**Image References**

12019. (2013, Jan. 30). *World War II allies* [Image]. Pixabay. https://pixabay.com/photos/world-war-ii-allies-generals-76645/

Gigglekid. (2014, Sept. 2). *Bomber aircraft* [Image]. Pixabay. https://pixabay.com/photos/bomber-war-aircraft-airplane-world-429985/

JacekAbramowicz. (2016, Feb. 11). *Auschwitz-Birkenau concentration camp* [Image]. Pixabay. https://pixabay.com/photos/auschwitz-birkenau-concentration-camp-1187918/

Simon_Goodall. (2022, Jan. 11). *Winston Churchill* [Image]. Pixabay. https://pixabay.com/photos/churchill-winston-britain-scotland-6924619/

tislas. (2018, Nov. 21). *Iwo Jima military flag monument* [Image]. Pixabay. https://pixabay.com/photos/iwo-jima-military-flag-monument-3820507/

TomaszProszek. (2014, Nov. 28). *World War II plane* [Image]. Pixabay. https://pixabay.com/photos/the-plane-world-war-2-flight-sky-548378/

WikiImages. (2012, Dec. 21). *Cologne bombing* [Image]. Pixabay. https://pixabay.com/photos/cologne-bombing-destruction-war-63176/

WikiImages. (2013, Jan. 3). *Normandy supply Second World War* [Image]. Pixabay. https://pixabay.com/photos/normandy-supply-second-world-war-67545/

WikiImages. (2012, Dec. 5). *Bernard Montgomery* [Image]. Pixabay. https://pixabay.com/photos/war-world-war-bernard-l-montgomery-62848/

WikiImages. (2012, Dec. 21). *Normandy landing craft* [Image]. Pixabay. https://pixabay.com/photos/war-landing-craft-normandy-63137/